Love
in Action

OTHER BOOKS BY THICH NHAT HANH

Be Free Where You Are

Being Peace

Call Me by My True Names

Calming the Fearful Mind: A Zen Response to Terrorism

Fragrant Palm Leaves: Journals 1962–1966

Good Citizens: Creating Enlightened Society

Interbeing: The Fourteen Mindfulness Trainings of
Engaged Buddhism

Keeping the Peace: Mindfulness and Public Service

Love Letter to the Earth

The Mindfulness Survival Kit: Five Essential Practices

Peace Begins Here: Palestinians and Israelis Listening to
Each Other

The Sun My Heart: From Mindfulness to Insight Contemplation

Touching Peace: Practicing the Art of Mindful Living

The World We Have: A Buddhist Approach to Peace and Ecology

Vietnam: Lotus in a Sea of Fire

Love
in Action

Writings on Nonviolent
Social Change

Including
*The Path of Return
Continues the Journey:
A Play in One Act*

SECOND EDITION

Thich Nhat Hanh

Foreword by
Brother Phap Huu

PARALLAX PRESS
BERKELEY, CALIFORNIA

Parallax Press
2236B Sixth Street
Berkeley, CA 94710
parallax.org

Parallax Press is the publishing division of Plum Village Community of Engaged
Buddhism
© 1993, 2024 Plum Village Community of Engaged Buddhism

Cover design by Katie Eberle
Interior design by Happenstance Type-O-Rama
Cover photograph © Plum Village Community of Engaged Buddhism

Printed on recycled paper in Canada

Library of Congress Cataloging-in-Publication Data is available upon request

1 2 3 4 5 FRIESENS 26 25 24 23 22

CONTENTS

The Path to Transforming Generational Suffering and Hatred

BROTHER PHAP HUU

My teacher, Zen Master Thich Nhat Hanh, or Thay (Vietnamese for "teacher"), knew that violence does not end violence, killing does not end killing, and war does not end war; all they create is generational trauma. As a Buddhist monk, he did not take sides. Peace and nonviolence was his sole path. Today, thirty years since the first publication of these collected writings on nonviolent social change and peace activism, we once again have a chance to reflect on his teachings as a source of inspiration and hope for the present and future generations who dare to embrace peace and nonviolence in the face of the complex challenges and conflicts our world is experiencing.

The mindfulness practices Thay taught, which have manifested throughout the world in many forms, all begin with awareness of the breath as an anchor to help us come home to ourselves: first, to acknowledge the suffering within us, to generate the capacity to listen to it, and to hold space for it to transform. Thay's focus as a meditation teacher was to help us look deeply at the suffering in us *and* around us, knowing that such looking would show us a way out—a way to put love into action.

As his attendant for seventeen years, I observed that the foundation of Thay's actions was rooted in peace, true love, and right mindfulness. He illuminated the connection between peace within ourselves and peace in the world to allow us to see and understand conflict in a new light, bridging our personal healing and societal healing in the present moment. I learned from Thay that all our actions of body, speech, and mind can cultivate a foundation of internal peace that serves as a sustaining and impactful source of energy for the world around us. "Peace in oneself, peace in the world" is a calligraphy that I have seen my teacher write many times.

Thay was well aware that healing and transformation does not arise in isolation from social change. When there is war, violence, pain, and death in front of us, as there is right now, we may have feelings of anger, sadness, injustice, despair, and even hopelessness. This suffering is not mine or yours alone. It is a collective emotion and experience we all share in the here and now. As mindfulness practitioners, first and foremost, we build the capacity to hold the truth of suffering. In my own practice, I recognize and embrace the violence and anger that has been present in me since childhood. My parents, victims of the American War in Vietnam, confronted profound uncertainties that led to feelings of despair and suffering. My parents fled the country as refugees and did everything in their capacity to ensure that I had a better future than their own. They transmitted all their hopes and aspirations to me and, at the same time, unknowingly transmitted their pain and suffering as well. Their pain and suffering became my own. Suffering and the practice of mindfulness has been a gift. Since I am able to recognize the pain and violence inside of me, I have the capacity to fully recognize and practice with the violence that exists outside of me.

As a young monk, when I recognized the seed of violence present in me, I knew I had work to do. Through Thay's wisdom I gained the courage to embrace that seed of violence like I would a crying baby. I learned to not fear it but to hold it tenderly, to understand it, and to transform it. The mindfulness practice is a source of courage that allows us to slow down and to look deeply at the fear and discrimination present inside ourselves. When we can sit with ourselves, recognize, be comfortable with, and love both the most magnificent parts of our being and the more uncomfortable truths that we embody, we give way for profound transformation. This transformation becomes a torch of wisdom in the world—because we have cultivated the capacity to be present for ourselves, for our joy, pain, and suffering, we are able to be present for the joy, pain, and suffering of others and of the world. When we can accept ourselves, we are more able to listen to others and change what may seem to be an impossible situation for the better. In this way, peace is not just a concept, it is an embodied practice that begins with us and how we relate to ourselves and the world around us.

I ask myself: With all the trauma of the current polycrises driven by climate change, with extreme weather events, changing weather patterns, famines, and wars forcing more people to leave their homes in search of a refuge, is peace even possible? Is it naive? Is it really possible to see the truth of what's needed and to respond with love rather than reacting with fear, separation, self-protection, and blame? Letting go of preconceptions, my response is this: it is possible if we give it a chance. Actions rooted in love and compassion are the only way to solve the crises in the world. It is through deep listening and tending—to our own suffering and the suffering around us—that a path of peace becomes possible.

In historical and current times as well as in our daily lives, we rarely give peace an opportunity. We only call for peace when violence and destruction arise. What Thay wrote so many decades ago remains powerfully relevant today: there is a need for ongoing deep listening between nations and groups. However long wars may take—that's how much time, and more, that we need to sit together, to practice deep listening, to restore our humanity, and to recognize our interdependence to realize that we do not need to destroy others so that we ourselves can exist.

If we create opportunities for nations, communities, and people with different views to practice deep listening and sharing, there will be change. We will be able to touch the insight of interbeing, which celebrates the beauty of diversity, the beauty of different cultures with all their languages, sciences, music, arts, heritages, and ways of life. If we start to see each other as flowers in the garden of humanity, as Thay liked to say, our ways of seeing start to transform—we start to care for and tend to that garden. We cultivate the seeds of peace and love that lie dormant in our hearts so that our collective garden can flourish. We realize that in the garden of humanity, there is space for all. It liberates us from the view that in order for us to thrive we must destroy the other. Such a view only creates more suffering.

This suffering, of course, is not limited to humans alone—it affects our whole planet. Mother Earth gives us all the conditions necessary for life. She gives and gives, and yet, we keep destroying her. There is an underlying notion that the land is there for us to take and use, but deep ecology unequivocally tells us we are not separate from our environment. The Earth, as I often heard Thay say, is not outside of us: the Earth is us. So when we destroy others to take land, we are destroying the planet, and we are destroying ourselves.

In these pages and through the example of his life, Thay reminds us that we must persist. If we fall into despair, we allow suffering and violence to win. Thay often shared a story from his years of leading the School of Youth for Social Services during the Vietnam war. During this particular instance, he and his young community were helping to rebuild villages that had been destroyed by blanket bombings. There was one particular village that had been bombed and rebuilt again and again and again. The third or fourth time this happened, when Thay mobilized his team of activists to go out and once again rebuild the village, a young student looked at him in despair and asked, "Thay, is this village worth rebuilding if we know that it will be bombed again?" In that moment, Thay shared that he also touched the seed of deep despair. When he recognized this, he took refuge in his mindfulness practice to stay stable. He focused on his breathing to anchor himself as he felt the strong emotions and sensations that were arising within him so that he could create space for an insight into a way forward. Thay teaches us that these feelings are real and natural, and the practice is to embrace them and not to allow them to overwhelm us. It is the mud that leads to the lotus. So, in response to his young student, his answer was simple: *Yes, it is worth it. We have to move forward.* The rebuilding itself is an expression of love in action. Our actions represent hope that there is still humanity. We will keep showing up again and again, for as long as it takes.

These moments of insight are like stars that shine most brightly when the sky is at its darkest. Do not underestimate the transmission of acts of kindness, love, and care, even if the fruits of our actions are not immediately apparent. Every action counts. Every loving action we offer to our loved ones, our community, our nation, and our world starts with a mindful breath, a smile, a loving thought, a moment of understanding. It starts with the courage to hold space, the courage to listen, the courage to speak, the courage to shine the light of awareness and understanding where there is ignorance, and the courage to love. Rather than focusing on the potential outcomes of our actions, our practice is to be present and to respond to the needs of the present moment. Focusing on what may be is a trap that can lead to despair. We can take care of the future by taking care of the present.

War, conflict, and acts of violence happening all over the world are bells of mindfulness for humanity and each one of us. Reflecting on this and asking myself what I can do, guided by the prescient words contained in this book, I see that my responsibility is to transform the seeds of discrimination, fear, hatred and violence inside of myself. Only then is it possible for fear to be transformed into connection, violence into peace, and hatred into love. This is our collective responsibility. As Thay writes in this book's namesake chapter, "The success of a nonviolent struggle can be measured only in terms of the love and nonviolence attained, not whether a political victory was achieved."*

Even if you only have five minutes, use those five minutes to cultivate peace for yourself and for the world. If you live for ten more years, it is your responsibility to cultivate peace for those ten years, to transmit a path of peace and a culture of peace. However much time you may have, use that time to contribute to the legacy of peace and humanity through our ways of being. This is our practice of transforming wars, including the wars that have not yet broken out, both within us and outside of us. We all have a lot of work to do to give peace a real chance.

_____

* page 47

Thay's words are thunderous: Now, wherever you are, don't take what you have for granted. You are enough. The path of peace begins with the transformation of your own wrong perceptions and views that divide us. It starts with you. Begin now. The time is now.

This book is your companion on the path.

With deep love and trust,

Brother Phap Huu
November 18, 2023
Plum Village Upper Hamlet
Thenac, France

PART I

The Path of Return Continues the Journey: A Play in One Act, 1972

FOREWORD

Their Speech Is All of Forgiveness

A tone poem, a snatch of gentle, celebratory music. A verse about death, which is really about life. A transmutation of death; the emptying of the veins of death, the letting in of light and air to those fearful spaces. How does one cope with death, when death strikes, repeatedly, senselessly, destroying the young, the noble, the brave, the self-giving? Grief of course, a period of silence, space for mourning. Then afterward, a reassertion, acceptance. And finally, if one is lucky, endowed, perceptive, brave with the bravery of an artist and poet, it is possible to create something that faces the cruelty, the horror, and brings a "sea change" to that welter of blood, vengeance, cruelty, and deceit.

It is one of the classic and very nearly crushing ironies of the long war in Vietnam; we have been the recipient, time and again,

---

* Jesuit priest Daniel Berrigan and Thich Nhat Hanh met as anti-Vietnam War activists in the 1960s. Through a shared commitment to social engagement grounded in spiritual practice, they developed a close bond as fellow travelers on the path of peace. See *The Raft is Not the Shore: Conversations Toward a Buddhist-Christian Awareness* (Orbis Books, 2001) for additional context.

of gifts of the spirit, gifts of art, profound understanding, hope communicated, a definition of ourselves that exceeds by far our expectation of ourselves. We have heard time and again, from the "enemy," a stubborn distinction between ourselves as a people, and our leadership. Our people have been endowed (by presumption of the same "enemy") with compassion, political acuity, generosity, and goodness of spirit. We were a people saddled for a time with an unfortunate and cruel leadership, which persisted in bloodletting despite the best instinct of the majority. Thus went the reading of our character by our "enemy."

Such definitions have a mysterious power of creating what they signify, in a sense at least analogous to the sacramental. One thinks of such "opinions" so stubbornly held, so patiently reiterated over so long a period of violence, across such unexampled savagery, perpetuated by a whole succession of American leaders—one thinks of this, and is simultaneously appalled, exhilarated, and given hope. Is it possible that out of a persecuted, defamed, all but destroyed people should arise the Suffering Servant of our own oracles; possible that salvation for the heinous, blood-ridden West should once again come from the East—and this, not in times of social normalcy, but across the curtain of blood that we wove and suspended between that people and ourselves, upon which they were stretched and racked, day after day, the people to whom Pascal surely had reference, those "crucified until the end of time"?

In a universal catastrophe, it is surely presumptuous to single out one element, one tradition, as having "suffered more" than others. Who can measure such things? They stop the heart in its tracks. At the same time, the religious resistance in the US at the time of the Vietnam War could not help but take into special account, with a special gratitude, the Vietnamese Buddhist movement. Spiritually speaking, we were closest to them. We drew most fully on their tradition—such a stubborn, unwavering, gentle, persistent, resilient strength! It seems to me far from stretching a point (more likely simply making a point) to see in this Buddhist monk, Thich Nhat Hanh, and his people, a literal living out of the words of Paul the apostle, writing to his community, "fatiguing labors more abundant, imprisonments more frequent, lashings innumerable, many threats of death ... forty lashes less one ... three times scourged, once I was stoned, three times I suffered shipwreck; a night and a day I was adrift on the high seas; in frequent journey on foot, in perils from floods, in perils from robbers, in perils from my own nation, in perils from the Gentiles, in perils in the city, in perils in the wilderness, in perils on the sea, in perils from false brethren, in fatigue and hardship, in many sleepless nights, in hunger and thirst, in fastings, often in cold and nakedness.... And apart from these things, there is my daily pressing anxiety, my solicitude for all our communities!"

This monk, this suffering servant, who is also a poet, an activist, a teacher, and scholar, suffered a personal loss of the most appalling nature. Young Buddhists were studying at the School of Youth for Social Service (SYSS), which Nhat Hanh had founded in Saigon early in the '60s. There the students were imbued with the spirit of nonviolent service. On leaving the school, they were to go in groups to help the peasants of the South in whatever way possible—building homes, sowing or harvesting crops, resettling refugees, simple, concrete projects (we would even say, strikingly evangelical ones). But such a school, in such a time, became a mortal threat to some of those for whom weapons were the indispensable means of survival or liberation. A period of terrorism was quickly launched. Students were killed and maimed in a series of bombings. Finally, one night a horrendous crime unfolded. Five of the students were seized in their dormitories, led to the riverbank nearby, and shot. One survived, the others died immediately.

The episode was not widely reported around the world. It was merely another bloody stereotyped incident of war, a spurt of gunfire in the night, a cry, blood quickly shed, quickly erased. But not forgotten by a monk who was also the friend of the slain. And so after a time, after grief and loss had had their time, came this gift, this meditation of Nhat Hanh, peaceful and serious, theologically profound, hopeful, light, airy of spirit, a paschal death and victory, a passage by water from time to timelessness. Written, one may rightfully presume, by one whose soul already is compounded of these qualities, since he conveys them with such skill. Indeed, to him the dead are the quick, and violence is by no means the master, by no means speaks the last word, or stops the mouth of the victim, or indeed finally rules, whatever his boast, his bloodstained and inflated pretentions.

The ironies implicit in the play that follows are enormous and far of reach. We Americans cross the great waters with our techniques of death, supersonic instruments of appetite, great eyes and ears and maws, a deranged and decapitated sensory apparatus, to smell out and destroy the least lurking evidence of life, health, hope, tradition, faith, family, to tear out the very taproot of existence, to plow up and sow with salt that culture, thousands of years old, which has unfailingly nurtured a people. "Let it come down! Let it all come down!" is the manic whine of the Machine.

And lo, coming across those same waters (which we name consciousness, Styx, death, or primordial creation) comes another sort of craft, peopled with spirits, listening, bantering, remembering, laughing. Their wounds are healed, their memories lucid. They recall without rancor the method and moment of their death. If there is something new about them, it is a quality at once elusive, feisty, a way of standing within death, fronting it, mocking it gently, and perhaps, best of all, forgiving.

These spirits are as they were before death. And this is the genius of Thich Nhat Hanh. His dead have the verisimilitude of the living. They are young, they push shadows back instead of joining them. They push the dark back, they create space, they speak up. Very different indeed from the dimwit ghosts of Virgil's underworld; more like the robustness, the crudity, of Dante's people—those in hell, chiefly.

And yet with a difference, which continues to escape my mind. It has something to do with a work of authentic Buddhist art, by a monk, about his people. A quality of inwardness, almost of austerity; a patience that escapes our monitors and timepieces; a serenity, caricatured cruelly in the West as stoicism, before death. Something of the twice born, the resurrected, something one sees more and more rarely in the West; now and again in the faces of the old, in a few children, in the cruel ecstasy of street violence; a light within, struck and then out.

Only here it is a steady flame. It lights those bodies, making lamps of them, as they cross the waters in our direction. They come toward us, and their speech is all of forgiveness, of hope, and joy. Indeed, the play seems to me a simple act of forgiveness and reconciliation. Are you saying to us, Nhat Hanh, that the Vietnamese dead will come back to us who murdered them? Will come, not as ministers of vengeance, but sacramental presences, angels, spirits of new creation?

I hope so, with all my heart.

And I thank you, Nhat Hanh, monk, medium, necromancer, artist. For your grief, for your long travail, your exile, for the deaf and dumb and uncaring world, for the crucifixion and death of your people. Forgive us.

And because the monk Thomas Merton said it to you, and your play says it to me, I dare to repeat: Alleluia! We shall see his face!

Love Enables Us

At 12:30 a.m. on July 5, 1967, in the village of Binh Phuoc, Gia Dinh Province, Southeastern Vietnam, a group of strangers abducted five young men, brought them to the bank of the Saigon River, and shot them. All five were volunteer workers in the School of Youth for Social Service, a nonviolent organization that sought only to heal the wounds of war and reconstruct the villages. Their names were Tuan, Tho, Hy, Lanh, and Dinh. Tuan was a Buddhist novice.

Four died immediately. The fifth, Dinh, survived, but his clothes were soaked with blood, and he lost consciousness. The strangers thought all five were dead, so they left.

Silence on the river. There are many stars in the sky, but no moon. A small sampan comes gently to the shore. Mai appears. The sampan is large enough to take the four, only four, because the fifth, Dinh, is still alive, and must stay behind.

The author has said, "I guarantee that everything in this story is true." What story is he talking about? Is it the story of the five young men shot on the bank of the Saigon River? Everyone knows this is true—why does he have to guarantee it? Or is the author talking about what happened after the killing, about Mai with the sampan and the five of them rowing with their bare hands?

True or not, we will never know. But if the author has guaranteed it, then let us believe him. Listen to what he has said: "I remember when I first picked up my pen to write this play. I saw fourteen eyes looking at me, fourteen eyes wide open. I have said that I guarantee the story to be true. But what does it mean to be true? Who can be my witness?

"I have said that it is true because I have lived the life of the story. No scientific instrument can verify the existential nature of life in this story.

"Love enables us to see things that those who are without love cannot see.

"Who will be gone and who will stay? Where do we come from and where will we go? Are the other shore and this shore one or two? Is there a river that separates the two sides, a river that no boat can cross? Is such complete separation possible? Please come over to my boat. I will show you that there is a river, but there is no separation. Don't hesitate: I will row the boat myself. You can join me in rowing too, but let us row slowly, and very, very quietly."

CAST OF CHARACTERS

All the characters were real persons, and all the events are true.

VUI: a student of the School of Youth for Social Service (SYSS), Saigon.

LIEN: a teacher of the Tran Quy Cap High School, Hoi-An, and a political prisoner just released from jail. Volunteered her services to SYSS.

These two young women were murdered on the night of April 24, 1967, during a terrorist raid on the school by a group of unknown persons.

MAI: a young nun who had worked for the SYSS. One of the first ordained Tiep Hien (Order of Interbeing) sisters.* She immolated herself for peace on the night of May 16, 1967, at the Tu Nghiêm Pagoda in Saigon.

---

* The Order of Interbeing—Tiep Hien in Vietnamese—is a community of monastics and lay people who have committed to living their lives in accord with the Fourteen Mindfulness Trainings. These trainings are a distillation of the Bodhisattva (Enlightened Being) teachings of Mahayana Buddhism. The first six members of the Order, ordained together on February 5, 1966, were colleagues and students of Thich Nhat Hanh who worked with him to relieve the suffering of war through projects organized by the School of Youth for Social Service.

HY: a graduate of SYSS.

LANH: a graduate of SYSS.

THO: a graduate of SYSS.

TUAN: a young Buddhist novice, graduate of SYSS.

These four young men, all under twenty-five, were murdered on the morning of July 5, 1967. They had come to Binh Phuoc Hamlet, on the bank of the Saigon River, to work to improve the lot of its inhabitants.

VAN: a staff member of the SYSS—still alive in this world.

DUC: a staff member of the SYSS—still alive in this world.

PHUONG: a staff member of the SYSS—still alive in this world.*

DINH: a coworker of Hy, Lanh, Tho, and Tuan.

THE PRAJÑAPARAMITA (HEART) SUTRA: the Buddha's teachings on the interconnectedness (emptiness) of things and people.

---

* Cao Ngoc Phuong, later known as Sister Chan Khong, is the cofounder of Plum Village.

The Path of Return Continues the Journey

A Play in One Act

The story begins at 1:00 in the morning, shortly after Hy, Lanh, Tho, and Tuan were shot on the riverbank. Starry sky, no moon.

MAI: Let's sit so that the boat stays balanced. I'll sit in the bow. Tho, can you move over a little, near me. That's fine. Now we can start to row. Let's all use our bare hands. Gently, Tho! You're splashing all over me!

HY: We're going quite fast, aren't we, Sister Mai?

MAI: Yes. We're very light. Brother Tuan, look at Tho! He's waving his arms around too much and the boat is rocking back and forth. Please tell him to stop, will you?

THO: I'm not afraid of Tuan. I was a devil alive and I'm a devil dead. Okay, I'll keep quiet, but don't scold me!

TUAN: Tho, you are a little devil, but a lovable little devil. When we were alive, I used to knock on your head now and then, and for good reason. Sister Phuong said you were very bright. I don't know if that's true or not, but you certainly had the hardest skull in the world. I hurt my knuckles knocking on it.

THO: Brother Tuan, you hurt your knuckles because you behaved so badly! Look at Sister Mai. She never hurt her knuckles because she never knocked me on the head. Now that we're both dead, there is no way to find out whether my head was hard or your hand was soft.

MAI: Please, Tho, be quiet. I can see that you are quite bright. But please sit still! It's too difficult to row with you fidgeting like that. We've got hours to go.

HY: Are we really going to see Sister Lien?

MAI: Yes, Sister Lien and Sister Vui.

THO: What are they doing up there, Sister Mai?

MAI: Vui is still working for the villagers. And she has also taken up drawing. Lien just takes it easy—walking, reading the Heart Sutra, giving Vui drawing lessons.

THO: Sister Mai, how can Vui still work for the villagers after being killed?

MAI: Anywhere there are men and women—hell, heaven, wherever there are villages—Vui can work for the villagers. The last time I saw her she was pasting labels on the bottles of the mold they use to grow straw mushrooms.

THO (teasingly): She is probably growing the mushrooms to sell to the people in the hamlet. Vui should just wander about and enjoy herself. She already spent so much of her earthly life working for the villagers.

MAI: Vui has never been concerned about having fun the way you are! She is grown up, you know.

THO: I'm not a little boy. I'm only two years younger than Vui. I worked hard for the villagers too! If I hadn't, would I have been elected head of the Binh Phuoc camp?

MAI: We know you worked hard, but I still think you're not as grown up as Vui.

THO: Please stop teasing me, Sister Mai.

HY: Why do you keep playing Sister Mai's baby brother like that, Tho? Head of the Binh Phuoc camp! Some head! How you went around winning respect is beyond me.

THO: I don't care for anybody's respect. When we were alive, I used to act up a bit now and then to try to win your respect, but now that I'm dead, why should I bother? Brother Hy, tell me, are you sorry, I mean, are you sorry about being dead?

HY: What a question! Joy and sorrow are the affair of the living. Come on now, let's row a bit harder, and listen to this:

(Hy sings)

> Listen to me
> as you would to the song of the brook or the song of the bird,
> as you would look on the green weeping cherry,
> the pink roses, the yellow chrysanthemums, the violet bamboo,
> the white clouds, the bright moon.

(Faint sounds of little waves slapping against the sides of the boat)

THO: Wherever Hy goes he brings music and poetry along. What was that song? It sounds familiar.

MAI: Do you think you understand the song, Tho?

THO: Sister Mai, now that we're dead, what will we do? Do I have to keep working for the villagers like Vui?

MAI: No, you can do as you please. You can wander around and enjoy yourself.

THO: Great! Then maybe I'll be like Lien. That's what she does. But you said that she also studies the Heart Sutra and gives Vui drawing lessons.

MAI: That's right, you may do anything you please, just like Lien.

THO: But why does Vui have to work for the villagers?

MAI: I didn't say she had to. If Vui wants to do that, there is work for her to do. The universe of the dead changes according to your wishes. As I see it, the universe of the living does, too.

TUAN (in a low voice, to himself): The mind is like a painter. It can paint anything it wants.

THO: There goes Tuan and his Buddhist philosophy! Sister Mai, what is this world we are in now? Heaven or Hell? As far as I can see, it's not different from the world of the living.

MAI: It is neither Hell nor Heaven, Tho. And it's not as far away from the world of the living as people generally believe.

LANH: For that matter, the world of the living is not far from Heaven and Hell. Wouldn't you agree, Sister Mai? I feel that if I sing now, the living will hear me.

MAI: Well, at last we hear something from you, Lanh. You've been so quiet. Yes, you are right. The saying "Yin and Yang are irrevocably separate" is misleading. A lot of the sorrow that plagues the living comes from their belief that the two worlds are unbridgeable. Indeed, you can sing for the living, as I have many times ... as Hy just did.

THO: Hy used to be head of the Performing Arts Committee. Tell me, Hy, when we were alive, art was a means for building up the fabric of village life again after the destruction from war. We used poetry, painting, music, and theater to help people. How shall we use them now?

HY: When we were alive, art was with us. Now, art is still with us. Perhaps we are still alive, in some way. While we were living, we were already dying. How could we have life without death, or, for that matter, death without life?

THO: You're beginning to sound like Brother Tuan.

TUAN (clears his throat): And just what does that mean?

THO: Like a philosopher.

MAI: But, Tho, you sound like a philosopher, too. We all do. We always do when we become aware of something. Now that we are dead, we are much more lucid.

TUAN: This feels like the Saigon River. Is this still our country, our land, our water?

MAI: Yes, you only died last night, on the bank of this very river, eight kilometers back. I came immediately with this boat to get you. Now we are going upstream, toward the frontier.

(A long silence)

TUAN (*smiling faintly*): It's funny, I feel as if we died a long time ago. When I saw you coming, I felt as if I were waking up from a long, deep sleep. Now, I'm really quite awake.

THO: I wasn't surprised at all when I saw you, Sister Mai. It seemed the most natural thing in the world for you to be there. If you hadn't come, who would have?

MAI: It's true, I would always make time for all of you, no matter how busy I am.

LANH: If you hadn't come, we would still be sitting on the river-bank, waiting. If we had thought of you and wanted to find you, we wouldn't have known where to look.

MAI: If you had thought of me, you would have seen me coming. As I said a while ago, all things happen here according to our wishes.

LANH: It's strange. I don't feel any sorrow, pain, or bitterness. Sister Mai, I thought we would have these feelings, even after death. The living always tell stories about people who die unjustly. They talk about the revenge of the dead, and they become deathly afraid. Now I see that the dead are calmer and more lucid than the living. We dead do not think at all about vengeance. We just feel compassion for the living, even for those who killed us.

THO: If I were alive, I would go to the home of the man who killed me to ask him why he dragged me to the riverbank in the middle of the night and shot me. But I don't hold any grudge against him, none at all.

HY: Perhaps we dead are more forgiving because we no longer have to bear the heavy burden of our bodies and all our feelings of hate, anger, and desire. Desire and anger need a home, and now that we no longer have a body....

MAI: But Hy, how can you say that we no longer have a body? How could I see you if you didn't have a body? Our bodies are no longer heavy, no longer a burden, that's all. See how small and delicate this boat is, and yet it carries all five of us with ease.

THO: You're right! We really *are* light. The boat carries us and even moves quickly. Tell me, Sister Mai, were you there when they shot us?

MAI: No. But I had an intuition that something was wrong, so I brought the boat to get you. When I arrived, the four of you were still sitting on the riverbank. Hy's clothes were soaking wet, and he was shaking a little.

HY: When they shot me, I fell into the river. Because my arms were tied behind me, I could only use my feet to try to come up to the surface again, but they kept shooting until I sank completely.

MAI: Oh, Hy....

HY: Please don't feel sorry for me, Sister Mai. Save it for those who are still alive. I only had to endure a few seconds, a short minute of pain, that's all. But those close to us, who are still alive, they are the ones who suffer. Even those who killed us. They don't realize what they've done.

MAI: Tell me, Hy, what exactly happened?

HY: It was about midnight. Tuan, Lanh, and I were asleep at the Medical Post when a group of armed men arrived. They tied our arms behind us and set the Post on fire. The flames made it look as bright as day. Then they took us to the lake near the Tinh Vo gymnasium and told us to wait. A moment later, two more men arrived with Dinh and Tho. Their arms were also tied behind their backs. Then they took all five of us to the riverbank. We were next to the bamboo grove, supposedly waiting for a boat. Again and again, they asked if we were part of the Youth for Social Service, to be absolutely sure. Then, suddenly, they shot us. We four died, but Dinh was only wounded. They thought he was dead too, so they left.

TUAN: There were eleven of them. Some were very young, sixteen or seventeen. The oldest must have been under thirty. Some of them wore black clothes, some wore uniforms. One had a raincoat and another a poncho. Some wore military caps and bullet belts. I know who they were.

MAI: I know who they were, too. You don't have to say.

HY: I had the feeling they were not experienced at the business of killing. They had to kill us, but I could feel their reluctance.

THO: They obviously had orders from someone. The leader of the group, the one who shot me in the head twice, looked as though he had to convince himself to pull the trigger. He just didn't have it in him to do it easily. When they arrived at the house of the village medical chief, they immediately tied us together so we couldn't run. On the way to the river, we had to jump over two ditches about a meter wide, and at the second one, Dinh fell and they helped him up. I asked if they would cut us loose from each other so we could walk more easily, and they did. While we were walking, they talked to us in a very friendly way.

LANH: The men who abducted the three of us behaved the same way. They were very gentle. They let us stop and rest a couple of times. I really thought it wouldn't be too bad. When Tho crawled under barbed wire and cut himself, one man touched the wound on his forehead and asked about it, as a brother would. Another even patted me on the shoulder.

HY: And then they killed us.

MAI: What a pity! Men are such pitiful creatures.

HY: Sister Mai, you know I didn't say that with any blame. My eyes are now open. I see clearly now. I only hope that men discover a better way to be.

MAI: If anyone is tired, you can change your rowing hand. Just change seats with the person next to you. Tho, why don't you move over there and let Brother Tuan sit here. Good, let's go on. But take it easy, there's no hurry. The stars are so bright. You know, Hy, the eyes of the living have a difficult time seeing the whole of life.

HY: Isn't there a way to change that?

MAI (*speaking very slowly*): Man has progressed some, but so slowly. That is why, with our present consciousness, time in the living world goes so fast. Tell me, Brothers, before they shot you, did they say anything in particular?

LANH: They asked us if we were part of the School of Youth for Social Service. Then they walked a little ways away and whispered to each other. After that they approached us again and asked the same question, and then they consulted each other again in whispers. They repeated this a few more times, then they asked us, "Do you have anything to say?" When I heard that, chills ran up my spine. Tho said we had nothing to say, and then the leader touched Tho's forehead and said, very quickly, "I have to kill you." Then he put his gun to Tho's temple and fired two shots. The rest of us were shot right after. Hy fell into the river and was shot until he sank.

MAI: Poor Hy. Brother Van will be shattered when he hears about this.

TUAN: Yes. All those close to us will feel the loss. There is one consolation. (*He smiles*) The living forget quickly. In just a few months, the pain in their hearts will be soothed. Other worries and sorrows will help them forget. How could they go on living and working if they did not forget?

MAI: Still, I feel sorry for them. Some will record their love and pain on bricks and stones, or on paper with ink, to help themselves remember. But the only important image of the departed is the one that remains in the heart. As far as I am concerned, I pray that all those who were dear to me would forget me quickly so that they will not have to suffer any longer.

TUAN: Tho! What are you doing now?

MAI: Oh, no! He has regressed to his childhood. Watch out, dear Tho! You are tipping the boat!

THO: Now that I can become a child or a young adult as I wish, I do not long for my childhood anymore.

TUAN: Come back, Tho, to the Tho of twenty-one. I never met the Tho of eight. Please come back at once.

THO: All right, here I am. Brother Tuan, you are still quite bound by appearance. Don't you remember, it says in the Sutras, "It is not possible to recognize the Buddha by his physical appearance?" Since you were studying to be a fully ordained monk, you should be able to see me in any form. Why must I be only the Tho of twenty-one?

TUAN: Okay! Don't preach to me about the Diamond Sutra. Tho, do you really think that I cannot transform myself into a little child just as well as you? I am only afraid that if I did, you would be on your knees, begging your old Tuan to come back again.

THO (*laughing*): You're the one who was studying to be a monk, not I! It is only natural that I would *not* recognize you in the form of an eight-year-old.

MAI: Oh please, Tho, stop teasing Brother Tuan and sit still. Tuan, do you remember the exact moment you were shot?

TUAN: When I saw they had shot Tho, I recited the name of Amitabha Buddha, and right away I was riddled with bullets. I died quickly and felt no pain at all. What happened to Dinh?

MAI: He is still alive, Tuan. One bullet went through Dinh's arm and lung and punctured his pancreas. I bent down to look at him. The strangers had already gone, and Dinh was still conscious. He coughed over and over, and each time blood spurted out. His shirt was completely soaked in blood, but he will be rescued in time, don't worry.

THO (*thoughtfully*): When he is well again, he will tell our friends what happened. I wonder if he will remember anything to tell.

LANH: Maybe it would be better if he didn't remember anything. We died for tolerance and love, not for more hate and destruction.

MAI: I have faith in Brother Van and our friends. I have faith in all our brothers and sisters still living. They have refused and will always refuse to choose the road of violence.

(*A long silence, followed by flare bombs exploding on the riverbank, illuminating the water*)

Hy: They fire flare bombs all night, don't they!

Lanh: If they could see the dead, they would know we are rowing leisurely on the river. And they would hear the sound of the water lapping against the side of our boat in the dead of night.

Hy: They don't see us only because they don't think of us. If our beloved Brother Duc were there on the riverbank, he would see us and wave. Sister Mai, why does our country go on bleeding? When will this fire burn itself out?

Mai: Be calm, Brother. Our country will be destroyed, and our people will suffer even more than they already have. The cycle must be completed. Life and death are in the course of things. In the end there will be peace.

(Gun sounds from all sides)

THO: Some shooting! You know, Sister Mai, my mother can't sleep when she hears the guns.

MAI: Is she living by herself? Doesn't she have any children living at home?

THO: She is bringing up a small niece and they sleep in the same bed. But I am her only child.

HY: I heard that your father died a violent death also. Who killed him, Tho?

THO: When I was a child, I knew vaguely that he worked for the revolution. But let's not talk about this now. Mai, you said a while ago that Vui is working for the villagers. I still don't understand.

MAI: You will. Don't expect to understand everything in a single night. I'll show you Vui's village. She has many children in her school. Her village also has water buffalo, oxen, rivers, and many trees—banana, lemon, and mandarin.

LANH: Then I too will go on working for the villagers. I remember the lemon trees. But Sister Mai, you still have not told us *your* story. What have you done since you left us?

HY: Yes, you sacrificed yourself for the cause of peace such a long time ago. How many years has it been since then, Sister Mai?

THO: Years! It's only been a few months, hasn't it?

MAI: Everyone has his own notion of time. For me, it isn't a matter of months or years. It was lifetimes ago, generations ago.

THO: Tell me, Sister Mai, was the fire very hot?

MAI: What a question! I only remember that I was calm. And my wish was fulfilled. Before the moment arrived, I prayed I would be able to sit still in the fire. I sat very still.

LANH: When we heard the news, we cried like babies. We thought you left us because you didn't care about us.

MAI: Don't say that, Brother. There is no choice that doesn't involve suffering.

LANH: Oh, we were jealous of you. Remember that we were still living. We were jealous of your spirit and your act, that is all. I certainly understand it better now.

THO: Then where did you go, Mai?

MAI (*silent and thoughtful a long while*): I stood on the balcony looking down at my own body enveloped in flames. Yes, I think I even smiled, though my eyes were filled with tears. All the people standing around were weeping, and I wept with them. But when my father arrived, I didn't cry. That was the most difficult moment. Nothing can be more painful than seeing those dear to you suffer because of what you have done. I left long letters to my parents, asking them to understand. But, as you know, letters don't mean very much.

HY: Then what happened, Sister Mai?

MAI: My father fainted, regained consciousness, and then fainted again. Fortunately, an Army captain arrived and wanted to examine and confiscate my charred body. My father was so angry that he shook all over, and somehow, his anger subdued his pain.

THO: Three cheers for the captain!

MAI: Since then, I have had all the time in the world, and I have been very peaceful. My heart went out to each one of you. Many times, I came to aid and protect you. What happened tonight is different. It is destiny.

HY: What have you done since then?

MAI: I've gone to many places. Up the mountain, down to the sea. Don't you see? I'm still wearing white grapefruit blossoms in my hair. Even though my eyes have seen our ruined vegetable gardens and rice fields, my heart has been set free. I know that peace is coming. The wheel is turning in that direction. I've gone through entire regions where all the forests have been burned down, charred and black, where the bombs have crushed the earth and bulldozed the fields, making craters everywhere. And I've seen crowds of refugees carrying their meager possessions on their backs—babies, cooking pots, a few clothes—their steps uncertain, their eyes bewildered.

LANH: Can the dead do anything to help the living, Sister?

MAI (*laughs*): I died a long time ago, but I know I am not really dead. The voice and figure in front of you are only my voice and body in relation to yours. I'm still present in the world of the living, and there I go on with my work.

THO: Present in the world of the living? How can you be dead and, at the same time, present in the world of the living?

MAI: It's simple. I think Brother Tuan will explain it to you.

TUAN: Go ahead, Sister Mai, you explain.

MAI: If you set fire to a piece of charcoal, it burns red and becomes heat. When the fire dies, the charcoal is reduced to ash. Heat is the afterlife of the charcoal. From then on, the heat begins an uninterrupted process of influences, either in terms of energy or physical properties. And that process of transformation, like a chain reaction, takes place either directly or indirectly in relation to other processes of transformation.

TUAN: We call it "correlated reactions."

MAI: Yes, "correlated reactions." Nothing can be lost; yet at the same time, nothing can keep its nature intact.

HY: It's the same as when Tho became the eight-year-old he once was. Even though we did not recognize him, he was exactly himself.

MAI: Death is change, a sudden evolution, that's all. If Tho had died when he was eight, there wouldn't have been a Tho of twenty-one who was just killed and who's sitting here now. Actually, though, the eight-year-old Tho had to die, to give way to the twenty-one-year-old Tho. But the death of the eight-year-old Tho was not sudden. It was a progressive change, a process of slowly growing and transforming.

THO: One could also say it was a second-by-second evolution, while our own deaths tonight are an evolution of an entire life cycle.

MAI: That's more to the point than my explanation, Brother Tuan. That's it, Hy. In order to grow, Tho had to receive support from many other forms of existence—air for his lungs, food for his body, education for his mind, love for his heart. In Tho, there are innumerable beings—his father and mother, myself, and that girl with ruddy cheeks who will cry this morning over his departure. She should be sleeping peacefully now in the world of the living.

THO: I see, Sister Mai! You're saying I'm present in her now, too, and in all who love me in the world of the living. That's why I'm still there, and still able to provoke this chain reaction.

MAI: That's right. But you're not only present within them; you are present outside them as well. All you have said and done has already begun its journey. You are present everywhere.

LANH: Then what we see in front of us now is not all of Tho?

MAI: How can it be when already the Tho of twenty-one is no longer the Tho of eight? The Tho in front of us is only the Tho of the narrow world of our perceptions. He is merely our perception of Tho.

LANH (raising one finger): Sister Mai, first let me say something, then you tell me whether I'm right or wrong. We are rowing up the

Saigon River and telling ourselves that we're going to pay a visit to Lien and Vui. Actually, we're only going to see the Lien and Vui in the world of our own perceptions because their real existence is far greater. We only need to look around to see them everywhere.

MAI: That's right. We are going upstream in search of the Lien and Vui of our perceptions, of our habitual way of seeing them. That is why we have to struggle upstream to reach the frontier; in truth, our habits and feelings are even more present in the world of the living—their presence there is clearer and more substantial than in this world.

THO: Still, I would like to visit the village where Vui is working to see if she is doing better than last year. And I would like to see the lemon trees of my homeland again.

MAI: But no one is saying you can't. You will see Vui. You can even become a work coordinator here, you know.

THO: And Lien, where is she now?

MAI: She lives quite peacefully with Vui, smiling almost all the time. They are practically inseparable. The last time I saw her, she had the whole collection of the Maha Prajñaparamita Sutra in her hand. You know, she is reading the entire thing.

TUAN: If I read the Prajña Sutra now, I think I would understand it much more easily. There is such peace and calm within my heart.

MAI: When we see Lien, we have to ask her to explain the Prajña Sutra to us.

TUAN: When I was alive, not a day passed when I did not recite the Heart Sutra. I thought I understood it. But it was only when the man with the poncho pointed a gun at my head that I really saw what the Heart Sutra was all about.

LANH: Tell us, Brother Tuan, what did you see?

TUAN: It's hard to say, Lanh. It's not something to be understood, but to be *seen*. We can easily explain what we understand, but not what we see or perceive. It came all of a sudden, like lightning.

LANH (*begging*): But try, Brother Tuan, what did you see?

TUAN: Well, when that man with the poncho brought his gun up to my head, I realized immediately, without being aware of it consciously, that he was not going to shoot *me*. He was going to shoot something else, but not me. How could he shoot me without knowing who I was? Since then, I have been wondering how someone can blow the brains out of another without knowing them.

THO: You are funny, Brother Tuan! He asked us over and over again to make sure that we really were from the Youth for Social Service, before he killed us. He shot you because he *knew* who you were. You were a member of the Youth for Social Service. They wanted to kill the Youth for Social Service—therefore, they shot you.

LANH: Why are you smiling, Sister Mai?

MAI: Tho is speaking in terms of logic, and the Heart Sutra is exactly the tool we need to shatter that kind of reasoning.

TUAN: I agree with you, Sister Mai. "Youth for Social Service" is just a label that they pasted on the objects of their hatred or fear, an object that exists only in their perception. It has nothing to do with us as persons. They shot only at the object of their fear and hatred, but because they had labeled us as the object of their fear and hatred, they ended up shooting us, and we died by mistake. They killed us because they truly did not know who we were.

HY: Brother Tuan, are you speaking about wrong perceptions? Hatred and fear blind us; we no longer truly see each other. We see only the faces of imagined monsters, and that gives us the necessary courage to destroy each other.

MAI: The war raging in our homeland is caused by exactly this kind of blindness. Those who are shooting at this very moment do not know who they are fighting. All are victims. And some are ready to profit from the mutual destruction.

LANH: That is certainly true of those who killed us. For a fleeting moment, I think they saw that we were just human beings, not monsters. But, when the moment arrived, they had to shoot, to obey orders. It must be the cruel, irrevocable order imposed on man's destiny.

THO: Oh, Lanh, you talk as if there were such a thing as an abstract order. That order came from their superiors, who else?

MAI: You don't understand, Tho. The ones who killed you were only obeying the orders of their superiors. And those superiors were also victims. Yet, those who shot you did reveal their human qualities. They hesitated, not wanting to kill you, fighting against themselves. They carried out their orders because they were crushed between the hammer and the anvil, the orders and their families, their jobs, even their lives. Their consciences and perceptions had been greatly obscured.

HY: One man even exclaimed, "God, you are all so young!" It was not just an expression of pity for us but also a protest against his own fate.

MAI: Men kill because, on the one hand, they do not know their real enemy, and on the other hand, they are pushed into a position where they must kill. Let me tell you what happened to our Brother Duc last year. He was waiting for a civilian plane at a small isolated airport in the highlands, along with a young American army officer who was waiting for a caribou plane to fly him on a search-and-destroy operation. There was no one else besides the two of them. The young American struck up a conversation with Brother Duc, who immediately saw that the man knew nothing about Vietnamese history or culture or the truth of the conflict in which he was playing a part. He knew only one thing: the Vietcong were his enemy. His duty, as he put it, was to destroy the Vietcong in order to save the Vietnamese and the free world. Brother Duc felt so sad. He asked the GI, "Are you afraid of the Vietcong?" With that question, the soldier leaped to his feet. Duc saw the alarm and suspicion in his eyes, fear that Duc himself might be a Vietcong. The GI had been told again and again that the VC were very cunning, and wherever he went, he imagined that the VC were present. So he asked rapidly, putting his hand on his gun, "Are you a VC?" Brother Duc thought the question was funny, but he dared not smile. He knew that if he jokingly said "Yes," the soldier would shoot him. So he answered "No," and explained that he was only a professor of religion waiting to catch a plane back to Saigon. Do you know what our Brother Duc said after he told us about this incident? He said that if he had been killed then, it wouldn't have been because the American soldier wanted to kill him. The soldier only wanted to kill Vietcong, who he could hate only because he didn't really know what they were. He imagined that they were wild, cruel monsters that had to be hunted down and eradicated. In his country the people are fed so much of this that they keep letting their government send men over here to kill and be killed. So, men kill unjustly and in turn are killed unjustly, and it is their own countrymen who kill them. They are the ones responsible for the massacre of our people, but they think they have nothing to do with it because it is not they who hold the guns and pull the triggers. Who is really killing us? It is fear, hatred, and prejudice.

LANH: The world of the living is shrouded in fog. All I feel now is compassion for the destiny of mankind. It's like walking in a moonless, starless night.

MAI: Excuse me, but may I change the subject? You know, one of the reasons I'm taking you to see Sister Lien is that I want you to see her paintings. I believe she has really achieved something—in her earthly life she loved art very much, but now she has fully realized it. I am sure she draws inspiration from the Heart Sutra.

HY: Vui, too, used to love art when she was alive. I suppose they're in accord now. I love painting myself. Do you think I will understand Sister Lien's work? Inspiration drawn from the Heart Sutra, that's awesome!

MAI: What wouldn't you be able to understand, Hy? Just a while ago we discussed the Prajñaparamita itself! We each paint our own lives. If your work is broad and free, your life will be broad and free, also. That is all. We create our own worlds with our visions, conceptions, and thoughts. We might create a constricted world of suffering and sorrow, or one that is immense and free, a truly beautiful place. The essential ingredient is a spirit of openness, tolerance, and freedom.

HY: Now I understand what Brother Tuan meant when he said, "The mind is like a painter."

MAI (*laughs*): Yes. Why don't you all begin here and now to paint your own lives. Every artist is capable, through his art, of reaching the supreme objective of life itself.

THO: Then my picture, Sister Mai, will probably look like that of Vui. My world must contain a lemon tree! I once threatened Brother Duc that if the Pure Land has no lemon trees, I will refuse to enter! But that's not all. My world will also have coconut trees, moats where the water is clear in the morning, thatch-roofed schools where at noontime the children's singing reaches my ears: "Lam-Son Mountains! Lam-Son Mountains! Banners flapping in the wind!"

LANH: Tho, do be quiet! I didn't realize that the dead could be homesick! When little Thanh of Binh Phuoc Hamlet hears that his teacher has been killed, he'll cry until he has no tears left. Yes, our Pure Land must contain those little boys, and friendly meetings in the village where the first item on the agenda is always, "Our leader has a few words to say to you." There must also be those wharfs down by the river where we bathe, where we can swim over to the other side and snatch a few ears of corn to roast on an open fire and eat together. It's such a small world, isn't it, Sister Mai?

MAI (*smiles tolerantly*): No, Lanh, it is not a small world. The strokes of your painting are those of love. Not only scenes of mountains or clouds or immense skies are breathtaking. Lonely pines standing on snowy cliffs can also be free and bold. The world of the bodhisattvas also has lakes and ponds, low hills, curved bridges, and red earthen paths.

LANH (*mysteriously*): And highways.

MAI: Yes, and highways. Because of love, you draw lemon trees, fig trees, bamboo groves, and river wharfs. The longer the war lasts, the more hatred it creates, and love is being crushed underfoot. We see those dear to us unjustly destroyed and it is hard to keep our hearts peaceful so that love can survive. Using hatred to fight hatred is the surest way to create even more hatred. Those who create love are fewer and fewer, while those who create hate are more and more. And we are changed by it all. Simple, honest, close-to-the-earth people, even after the war is over, will go on bearing the deep wounds inflicted by all this hatred.

LANH: Isn't that the biggest concern? It must be better to be destroyed in a split second and then recreated than to destroy all faith and love.

TUAN: Yes, Lanh, that is our basic concern. I, myself, was born in 1945, the year of the revolution. The last of our family's three boys. As we grew up, all we saw was war and hatred. My hometown, Ben Tre, was where the energy and fervor of the revolution were in constant movement, much like the swift, deep water of the Tien Giang River on its way to the sea. Fortunately, my family realized early on the necessity of love and encouraged me to follow my inclination for a monk's life. I went to the Buddhist institutes of Giac Sanh, Tra Vinh, and later An Quang. Then I took up social studies and fieldwork. When I worked hard, it was not because I had any illusion about my ability to change the situation. That would have been like trying to extinguish a forest fire with a cup of water. But I did have faith then, and I still have faith now, that our work was of value because it sowed seeds of tolerance and love in people's hearts.

LANH: Let's hope that our earthly lives, as well as our deaths, have sown the seeds of tolerance and love. Sister Mai's death, for instance, did not provoke any hatred. On the contrary, it awakened in many people the ability to understand and sacrifice, even people far away.

MAI: We are approaching the source of the river, my brothers. Have you noticed how thick the forest is getting?

HY: The boat has been going fast, Sister Mai. Is Vui's village near the frontier?

MAI: Yes. In twenty kilometers, we will leave the boat for the jungle. The current will be so strong that it will be impossible for us to continue to row upstream.

(*Monkeys' cries echo through the forest*)

THO: Dawn is almost here, friends. Brother Tuan, look up at the great trees, pink in the light of dawn! There is someone standing there waiting, isn't there? Could it be Lien?

MAI (*smiles*): Of course it's Lien. Who else? Let's row a bit harder, come on, let's row.

PART II

Writings on Nonviolent Social Change

ONE

Love in Action, 1969

Thich Nhat Hanh played a central role in the Buddhist movement for peace in Vietnam during the 1960s and served as Chair of the Buddhist peace delegation to the Paris Peace Talks, which began in 1968 and would continue in deadlock for three-and-a-half years. His essay "Love in Action" was adapted from the booklet *Love in Action: The Nonviolent Struggle for Peace in Vietnam* (Paris: Vietnamese Buddhist Peace Delegation, 1969.

The essence of nonviolence is love. Out of love and the willingness to act selflessly, strategies, tactics, and techniques for a nonviolent struggle arise naturally. Nonviolence is not a dogma; it is a process. Other struggles may be fueled by greed, hatred, fear, or ignorance, but a nonviolent one cannot use such blind sources of energy, for they will destroy those involved and also the struggle itself. Nonviolent action, born of the awareness of suffering and nurtured by love, is the most effective way to confront adversity.

The Buddhist struggle for peace in Vietnam in the 1960s and '70s arose from the great suffering inflicted on our nation by international forces. Blood and fire ravaged the countryside, and people everywhere were uprooted. The Vietnam War was, first and foremost, an ideological struggle. To ensure our people's survival, we had to overcome both communist and anticommunist fanaticism and maintain the strictest neutrality. Buddhists tried their best to speak for all the people and not take sides, but we were condemned as "pro-communist neutralists." Both warring parties claimed to speak for what the people really wanted, but the North Vietnamese spoke for the communist bloc and the South Vietnamese spoke for the capitalist bloc. The Buddhists only wanted to create a vehicle for the people to be heard—and the people only wanted peace, not a "victory" by either side.

During our struggle, many scenes of love arose spontaneously—a monk sitting calmly before an advancing tank, women and children raising their bare hands against barbed wire, students confronting military police who looked like monsters wearing huge masks and holding bayonets, young women running through clouds of tear gas with babies in their arms, hunger strikes held silently and patiently, monks and nuns burning themselves to death to try to be heard above the raging noise of the war. And all of these efforts bore some fruit.

Any nonviolent action requires a thorough understanding of the situation and of the psychology of the people. In Vietnam, we inherited many ideas from the Buddhist tradition, and we learned from our mistakes as we went along. In the late nineteenth and early twentieth centuries, Buddhist monks joined the struggle for independence from the French, and they won the support of their countrymen. When the Vietnam War broke out, they still had that support, as well as the knowledge gained earlier to go beyond passive resistance and undertake positive efforts to overcome the war and the oppression. In 1966, when the people of Hue and Da Nang learned that

Field Marshall Nguyen Cao Ky* was about to bring tanks and troops from Saigon to suppress the movement for peace, the people of those cities brought their family altars—the most sacred objects in their homes—onto the streets, relying on their culture and tradition to oppose the forces of destruction. Some people were critical, saying they used religion for political purposes, but I do not agree. They were using their most potent spiritual force to directly confront the violence. This was not a political act; it was an act of love.

Fasting, the method used most by Mahatma Gandhi to help India in its struggle for independence, was also used in Vietnam. Sometimes, thousands of people fasted, and other times, a single person fasted. We fasted as prayer to purify our hearts, consolidate our will, and arouse awareness and compassion in others. When Thich Tri Quang fasted for one hundred days, those who passed the Duy Tan Clinic were jarred into awareness, and compassion was born in them. As a result, they felt compelled to meet, talk, and plan, thereby escalating the struggle. Thich Tri Quang had not *planned* to fast. He *had* to fast.†

---

* Nguyen Cao Ky (1930–2011), then Field Marshall, was a Vietnamese military officer and politician who served as the chief of the Republic of Vietnam Air Force in the 1960s, and became the prime minister of South Vietnam in a military junta from 1965 to 1967. Later he served as vice president to President Nguyen Van Thieu from 1967 to 1971.

† Thich Tri Quang (1923–2019) was a Vietnamese Buddhist monk who led South Vietnam's Buddhist population during the Buddhist crisis in 1963. His 1963 campaign, in which he encouraged followers to emulate the nonviolent example of Mahatma Gandhi, led to widespread demonstrations against the government of President Ngo Dinh Diem, who, together with his brother the Roman Catholic Archbishop of Huế, Pierre Martin Ngo Dinh Thuc, mistreated the Buddhists, who were in the majority. Violent crackdowns on Buddhist demonstrations and the self-immolation of at least five Buddhist monks in protest led to a US-backed military coup in November 1963 in which President Diem and Madame Nhu were deposed and assassinated.

We also used literature and the arts as "weapons" to challenge the oppression. Works by antiwar writers, composers, poets, and artists, although illegal, were widely circulated. Antiwar songs were sung in streets and classrooms, and antiwar literature became the largest category of books sold in Vietnam, even infiltrating army units. *Look Back at Your Homeland*, *Only Death Allows You to Speak Out*, and *Lotus in a Sea of Fire* sold hundreds of thousands of copies. Our literature was considered dangerous by both sides. One book of poems, *Let Us Pray so the White Dove Will Be with Us*, was submitted to the Ministry of Information, and only two of the sixty poems in it were approved. A group of students published it anyway, and within a week, all copies were sold. In Hue, a policeman saw a copy in a bookstore and warned the owner, "Hide this and only bring it out when someone asks for it." Sister Cao Ngoc Phuong* was arrested in Hue for transporting antiwar books, and before I left the country, I was also arrested and imprisoned for a few days in Bao Loc for "antiwar" activities, although I was charged only with the crime of listening to Hanoi Radio.

Folk poetry was used as a means of education. This lullaby was sung throughout the country:

> My hand is holding a bowl of ginger and salt.
> Ginger is hot, salt is strong.
> They embrace each other.
> North and South share the same sorrow.
> We love each other,
> why have we abandoned our love?

This "Prayer for Peace" was printed by the tens of thousands and chanted during religious services throughout Vietnam, and its effects were widely felt:

---

* Later known as Sister Chan Khong, the cofounder of Plum Village.

Homage to all Buddhas in the ten directions.
Please have compassion for our suffering.
Our land has been at war for two decades.
Divided, it is a land of tears,
and blood and bones of young and old.
Mothers weep till their tears are dry,
while their sons on distant fields decay.
Its beauty now torn apart,
only blood and tears now flow.
Brothers killing brothers
for promises from outside.

During the superpower confrontation in Vietnam, while thousands and thousands of peasants and children lost their lives, our land was unmercifully ravaged. Yet we were unable to stop the fighting; we were not able to make ourselves heard or understood. We had little access to the international news media. People thought we Buddhists were trying to seize power, but we had no interest in power. We only wanted to stop the slaughter. The voice of the Vietnamese people—80 percent Buddhist—was lost in the melee of shooting and bombs. But we realized that the means and the end are one, and we never employed any kind of action that betrayed our commitment to nonviolence.

In 1963, Venerable Thich Quang Duc went to the crossroads of Phan Dinh Phung, sat in the lotus position, poured gasoline on himself, and transformed himself into a torch.[*] His disciple read his last words to the press. Madame Nhu described it as a

---

[*] Thich Quang Duc (1897–1963) was a Vietnamese Buddhist monk who publicly self-immolated at a busy Saigon road intersection to protest the persecution of Buddhists by the South Vietnamese government. After Quảng Đức, five more Buddhist monks self-immolated that year as the Buddhist protests in Vietnam escalated.

"barbecue."* By burning himself, Thich Quang Duc awakened the world to the suffering of the war and the persecution of the Buddhists. When someone stands up to violence in such a courageous way, a force for change is released. Every action for peace requires someone to exhibit the courage to challenge the violence and inspire love. Love and sacrifice always set up a chain reaction of love and sacrifice. Like the crucifixion of Jesus, Thich Quang Duc's act expressed the unconditional willingness to suffer for the awakening of others. Accepting the most extreme kind of pain, he lit a fire in the hearts of people around the world. Self-burning was not a technique or program of action. When anyone wished to burn himself or herself, the Buddhist leaders always tried to prevent it. But many monks, nuns, laymen, and laywomen did sacrifice themselves for peace in this way, including my disciple Nhat Chi Mai, who declared that she wanted to be "a torch in the dark night."

Nhat Chi Mai was one of the first six people ordained into the Tiep Hien Order. In 1966, she placed a statue of Avalokitesvara, the bodhisattva of compassion, and a statue of the Virgin Mary in front of her, and burned herself alive at the Tu Nghiem temple, a nunnery. She left behind letters to the presidents of North and South Vietnam, imploring them to stop the fighting. She wrote one letter to me: "Thây, don't worry too much. We will have peace soon." Evoking the force of love, Nhat Chi Mai moved the hearts of millions of her countrymen.

I know that the self-immolation of monks and nuns was difficult for Westerners to understand. The Western press called it suicide,

---

* Madame Nhu was the de facto First Lady of South Vietnam from 1955 to 1963 as the wife of Ngo Dinh Nhu, the brother and chief advisor to President Ngo Dinh Diem.

but it was not really suicide. It was not even a protest. What the monks wrote in the letters they left behind was intended only to move the hearts of the oppressors and call the world's attention to the suffering of our people. To make a statement while enduring such unspeakable pain is to communicate with tremendous determination, courage, and sincerity. During the ordination ceremony in some Buddhist traditions, the ordinee burns one or more very small spots on their body with moxa incense as they take the twenty-five hundred vows of a monastic, promising to live a life devoted to helping living beings. If they were to say this while sitting comfortably in an armchair, it would not be the same. When uttered while kneeling before the community of elders and experiencing this kind of pain, their words express the full seriousness of their heart and mind.

The Vietnamese monks, nuns, and laypeople who burned themselves were saying with all their strength and determination that they were willing to endure the greatest of suffering in order to protect their people. But why did they have to burn themselves to death? The difference between burning oneself with incense and burning oneself to death is only a matter of degree. The importance was not to die, but to express courage, determination, and sincerity—not to destroy, but to create. Suicide is an act of self-destruction based on the inability to cope with life's difficulties. In Buddhism, self-destruction is one of the most serious transgressions of the precepts. Those who burned themselves had lost neither courage nor hope, nor did they desire nonexistence. They were extremely courageous and aspired for something good in the future. They sacrificed themselves in order to seek help from the people of the world. I believe with all my heart that those who burned themselves did not aim at the death of the oppressors but only at a change in their policy. Their enemies were not human beings, but the intolerance, fanaticism, oppression, greed, hatred, and discrimination that lay within the hearts of their fellow men and women.

We did not plan self-immolation or any of the other methods that were used. But confronting the situation and having compassion in our hearts, ways of acting came by themselves. You cannot prefabricate techniques of nonviolent action and put them into a book for people to use. That would be naive. If you are alert and creative, you will know what to do and what not to do. The basic requisite is that you have the essence, the substance of nonviolence and compassion in yourself. Then everything you do will be in the direction of nonviolence.

Besides self-immolation, fasting, and the use of art, literature, and culture, many other tactics were employed in Vietnam. Foreign Minister Vu Van Mau, for example, resigned in 1963 and shaved his head to protest the violent policies of the Diêm regime, and many professors and students followed suit. There were labor strikes at the harbors and markets, and business owners turned in their licenses. University deans, presidents, and professors resigned, and high school and university students boycotted classes and examinations. Draftees refused to fight. All of these acts were met with atrocious reprisals. The government used unbridled brutality—tear gas, suffocation gas, grenades, prisons, and torture—to obstruct and suppress these nonviolent efforts.

Police agents posed as monks and nuns and infiltrated our movement, damaging our prestige and sowing seeds of fear. They excited extremists and fanatics to overturn and destroy the leadership and members of the movement. No one knows exactly how many Buddhist and non-Buddhist leaders of the nonviolent movement were imprisoned or killed, including professors, students, intellectuals, politicians, workers, and farmers. Even social workers trying to help the peasants were terrorized and murdered. From the School of Youth for Social Service (SYSS), eight people were kidnapped, six killed, and eleven seriously wounded—all because they refused to take sides in the war. In a memorial service organized for those who were killed, the SYSS students openly affirmed their commitment to nonviolence and neutrality: "Now, in the presence of our dear friends whose bodies are lying here, we solemnly proclaim that we cannot consider you who killed them to be our enemies. Our arms are open wide; we are ready to embrace your ideas and advice to help us continue our nonviolent ways of working for the people of Vietnam."

Despite the results—many years of war followed by years of oppression and human rights abuse—I cannot say that our struggle was a failure. The conditions for success in terms of a political victory were not present. But the success of a nonviolent struggle can be measured only in terms of the love and nonviolence attained, not whether a political victory was achieved. In our struggle in Vietnam, we did our best to remain true to our principles. We never lost sight that the essence of our struggle was love itself, and that was a real contribution to humanity.

TWO

A Proposal for Peace, 1966

Thich Nhat Hanh read "A Proposal for Peace" at a press conference in Washington, DC, on June 1, 1966, and reprinted it in the United States Congressional Record the following day.

Just this morning, the US consulate in Hue was destroyed by angry Vietnamese youths. In the past four days, five Vietnamese have immolated themselves, some of them leaving behind messages explaining that their actions were in protest against US policy in South Vietnam. During my short visit to your country, I have been repeatedly asked why the Vietnamese people seem to have become so strongly anti-American.

I wish, first, to assure you that I am not anti-American. Indeed, it is precisely because I do have a great respect and admiration for America that I have undertaken this long voyage to your country, a voyage that entails great personal risk for me upon my return to South Vietnam. Yet I assume this risk willingly because I have faith that if the American public can begin to understand something of what the Vietnamese people feel about what is happening in our country, much of the unnecessary tragedy and misery being endured by both our peoples might be eliminated.

The demonstrations, self-immolations, and protests that we are witnessing in Vietnam are dramatic reflections of the frustrations that the Vietnamese people feel at being so effectively excluded from participation in the determination of their country's future. Eighty years of French domination over Vietnam were ended by a long and bloody struggle waged and won by the Vietnamese people against overwhelming odds.* During the twelve years since independence, most Vietnamese have remained without a voice in the nation's destiny, and this at a time when the nation is being subjected to a destructive force far surpassing anything ever before seen in our country. If anti-Americanism seems to be emerging as a focus for some of the recent protests, it is because the Vietnamese people recognize that it is only the awesome US power that enables the Saigon governments to rule without a popular mandate and to follow policies contrary to the aspirations of the Vietnamese people. This is not the independence for which the Vietnamese people fought so valiantly.

The war in Vietnam today pits brother against brother, the Vietcong against the supporters of the Saigon government. Both sides claim to represent the Vietnamese people, but in reality neither side does. The most effective Vietcong propaganda says that the Saigon governments are mere puppets of the US, corrupt lackeys of the imperialists.

---

* French Indochina was a grouping of French colonial territories in Southeast Asia—including the Vietnamese regions of Tonkin in the North, Annam in the center, and Cochinchina in the South—from 1867–1954. With the Geneva Agreements, after many years of conflict, France relinquished any claim to territory in the Indochinese peninsula.

Every escalation of the war, every new contingent of US troops, confirms these charges and wins new recruits to the Vietcong, for the overwhelming majority of the Vietnamese people now thirst desperately for peace and oppose any further expansion of the war. They see clearly that the present policy of constant escalation only puts peace ever further into the future and merely guarantees an even greater destruction of Vietnamese society. There are now more than three hundred thousand Americans in my country, most of them knowing and caring little about our customs and practices and many of them involved in destroying Vietnamese people and property.

This creates friction which generously feeds the anti-American propaganda, and the fact that the war kills far more innocent peasants than it does Vietcong is a tragic reality of life in the Vietnamese countryside. Those who escape death by bombings must often abandon their destroyed villages and seek shelter in refugee camps where life is even more miserable than it was in the villages. In general, these people do not blame the Vietcong for their plight. It is the men in the planes, who drop death and destruction from the skies, who appear to them to be their enemies. How can they see it otherwise?

The United States chooses to support those elements in Vietnam that appear to be most devoted to the US's wishes for Vietnam's future. But these elements have never been viewed by the Vietnamese people as their spokesmen. Diêm was not, nor were Diêm's successors.* Thus, it has been the US's antipathy to popular government in South Vietnam, together with its hope for an ultimate

---

* Ngô Đình Diệm (1901–1963) served as the first President of South Vietnam from 1955 until he was captured and assassinated during the 1963 military coup. His persecution of South Vietnam's Buddhist majority led to the "Buddhist crisis" of 1963.

military solution, that has not only contradicted the deepest aspirations of the Vietnamese people but actually undermined the very objective which we believe Americans are fighting for in Vietnam.

To us, America's first objective is to have an anticommunist, or at least a non-communist, Vietnam, whereas the Vietnamese people's objective is to have peace. They dislike communism, but they dislike war even more, especially after twenty years of fighting and bitterness, which has rotted the very fabric of Vietnamese life. Equally important, we now see clearly that continuance of the war is more likely to spread communism in Vietnam than to contain it.

The new social class of military officers and *commerçants* that has been created as a direct result of US involvement, a class of sycophants who support the war for crass economic reasons, are not the people to whom Washington should listen if it sincerely wishes to hear the voice of South Vietnam. The Vietnamese people reject with scorn this corrupt and self-seeking class that cares neither for Vietnam nor for the great ideals of America but thinks only of its own interests.

The opinion is often expressed that there is no alternative to the present US policy in Vietnam, neither on the political nor the military side. The non-communist alternatives to a military dictatorship are said to be too fragmented to offer a stable alternative, and a cease-fire and US withdrawal are considered unfeasible because it is feared that the Vietcong will take over the country by terror.

The Vietnamese people recognize both of these dangers, but they also recognize the utter futility of the present course and the catastrophic effects that it is having on our society. Furthermore, we do not agree that there is no alternative to a military dictatorship. The force of Vietnamese nationalism is such an alternative. Indeed, this is the sole force that can prevent the complete disintegration of South Vietnam, and it is the force around which all Vietnamese can unite. But nationalism cannot attain its effective potential in the present Vietnamese political climate, where opposition to the government invites open persecution upon oneself and identification with it discredits one in the eyes of the people.

More than a decade of this atmosphere has served to drive many of the Vietnamese nationalists into the National Liberation Front (NLF) or into an ominous silence. Last year, an effort by a prominent group of nationalists to circulate a mild petition requesting peace negotiations between the South Vietnamese government and the NLF was so brutally attacked by the government that we are not likely to hear from them soon again, despite their having attained some five thousand signatures in less than three days' time.

Today, the means for nationalist expression rests mainly with the Vietnamese Buddhists, who alone command sufficient popular support to spearhead a protest for popular government. This is not a new role for Vietnamese Buddhism, for in the eyes of the Vietnamese peasants, Buddhism and nationalism are inseparably entwined. The historic accident that made the popularization of Christianity in Vietnam coincident with France's subjection of Vietnam created this image.

The repression of our faith by the French and by President Diêm strengthened it. And today, with the Buddhist attempt to give expression to the long pent-up wishes of the submerged and ignored Vietnamese masses being met by the gunfire and tanks of the Vietnamese army, the Vietnamese people, Buddhist and non-Buddhist alike, clearly see whose actions reflect our national heritage and whose actions betray this heritage.

Thus, although the Vietnamese people may lose skirmishes because they have no foreign sources of support, the crude victories of the Saigon generals serve merely to weaken their credibility while confirming the Vietcong's propagandist claim that the government cares nothing about the people. The Buddhist efforts are designed not to weaken Vietnam's resistance but to create a genuine will to resist.

Differences do exist among the Buddhists, the Catholics, and the other sects, but they would not be unsurmountable if there were a climate in Vietnam that encouraged unity. But there are those who see a unified, popular, nationalist movement in Vietnam as a threat to themselves. Such persons help to sow disunity and then use the disunity which they create as a pretext for retaining power. No, we do not accept the evaluation that there is no alternative to the present type of government.

The second argument offered for continuing the present US policy is that a cease-fire and US withdrawal would merely leave Vietnam to the communists. This argument we must also reject. The Vietcong grow stronger because of the mistakes made by Saigon, not because of its communist ideology or its terror. If South Vietnam could achieve a government that was clearly responsive to the basic aspirations of the Vietnamese people and truly independent, the rebels would no longer have any basis for popular support. Indeed, the rebels would have lost their reason to rebel, and if any guerrilla activity were to continue, the Vietnamese people would have the will to resist it, for they could identify it as being hostile to Vietnamese nationalism, contrary to the people's longing for peace and reconstruction, and therefore of foreign inspiration.

Since coming to the United States, I have been asked repeatedly to outline concrete proposals for ending the strife in Vietnam. Although I am not a politician and cannot therefore suggest every detail of a satisfactory settlement, the general direction that such a solution must take is quite clear to me and to many of the

Vietnamese people. It does not involve the US in any negotiations with Hanoi, Peking, or the NLF. To the Vietnamese people, such talks, if necessary, are the proper province of Vietnamese officials.

My solution would be along the following lines:

1. A cessation of the bombing, North and South.

2. Limitation of all military operations by US and South Vietnamese forces to defensive actions: in effect, a cease-fire if the Vietcong respond in kind.

3. A convincing demonstration of the US intention to withdraw its forces from Vietnam over a specified period of months, with withdrawal actually beginning to take place as a sign of sincerity.

4. A clear statement by the US of its desire to help the Vietnamese people have a government truly responsive to Vietnamese aspirations and concrete US actions to implement this statement, such as a refusal to support one group in preference to another.

5. A generous effort to help rebuild, in light of the destruction that has been wrecked upon Vietnam, such aid to be completely free of ideological and political strings and therefore not viewed as an affront to Vietnamese independence.

Such a program, if implemented with sufficient vigor to convince the now understandably skeptical Vietnamese people of its sincerity, offers the best hope for uniting them in a constructive effort and for restoring stability to South Vietnam.

The plan is not perfect, for how can the US be sure that the South Vietnamese government and the Vietcong would cooperate in such a venture? As far as the South Vietnamese government is concerned, the past statements of Premier Ky have clearly indicated his unwillingness to seek a peaceful end to the war. In fact, it has been the contradiction between the aggressive words of Saigon and the peaceful statements of Washington that has so discredited the so-called US peace offensive of last winter. The withdrawal of the US support for Ky may thus be a necessary precondition for the implementation of such a plan.

It is obviously not possible to predict the response of the Vietcong to such a program, but the installation of a popular government in South Vietnam, plus a cease-fire and the beginning of an American withdrawal, would so undercut the Vietcong's position that it is likely to have no alternative but to cooperate.

Finally, if some may question why I ask the US to take the first step, it is because the US is militarily the strongest nation in the world. No one can accuse it of cowardice if it chooses to seek peace. To be a genuine leader requires not only big guns but also moral strength. America's history suggests that she has the potential to provide the world this leadership.

THREE

Our Green Garden, 1966

During the war in Vietnam, Thich Nhat Hanh's poetry was celebrated much in the same way as protest songs in the United States. Thich Nhat Hanh's writing and three of his poems were published in *The New York Review of Books* in June, 1966.*

In Vietnam, we take great risks publishing these poems. Buddhists who have protested the war have been arrested and exiled and now are being killed in Da Nang. It was because of this great risk that the Buddhists who demonstrated this spring were reluctant to advocate openly an end to the war through negotiations: instead, they called for elections and democracy. We have been placed in an impossible dilemma. If we openly call for peace, we are identified with the communists and the government will try to suppress us. If we criticize the communists, we find ourselves aligned with these Vietnamese who have been propagandists for the Americans for years

---

* These three poems—"Condemnation," "Our Green Garden," and Peace"—are found with other poems by Thich Nhat Hanh in *Please Call Me By My True Names* (Parallax Press, 2022).

and whose words against communism are soiled and discredited because they have been paid to say them. To be honorably anticommunist has been to remain silent, and being silent, we have been labeled innocent of the dangers of communism. But we are not. We are very well aware of the restrictions on Buddhism in the North. We have studied what has happened in China. We know there is no place for spirituality in Marxism. We are ready to undertake a peaceful political struggle with the communists, if only the destruction of the war can be stopped. We are confident that the South Vietnamese can protect themselves from communist domination if they are allowed to carry out their political life in peace.

The tragedy of American policy is that it has made such a peaceful political struggle very difficult. The Americans could have helped in reconstructing the country peacefully if they had cooperated with and strengthened the Buddhists and others who had the respect of the people. Instead, they tried to divide the Buddhists and prevent them from becoming an organized force, and this has been disastrous. Catholicism came to Vietnam with the French, and the Catholic leaders, backed by the US, were objects of suspicion for most of the people. The Buddhist tradition is closely linked with nationalism, and it is unthinkable to the broad mass of people that the Buddhists would betray them to a foreign power. At the same time, Vietnamese Buddhism is syncretic in character—there are Catholic priests who are closer to us on the question of peace than some of the older, more conservative Buddhist priests. (A few months ago, eleven Catholic priests issued a strong statement calling for peace, and they were attacked by the Catholic leaders.)

Now the US has become too afraid of the communists to allow a peaceful confrontation with them to take place, and when you are afraid, you cannot win. Sending three hundred thousand American troops to Vietnam and bombing the countryside has only caused the communists to grow stronger. American military operations have killed and wounded more innocent peasants than Vietcong, and the Americans are blamed and hated for this. The peasants are not violently antagonistic to the Vietcong. The strong anticommunists are mostly people in the cities who fear the loss of their property, cars, businesses, and homes and rely on the foreign army to protect them. The American soldiers, moreover, do not understand the Vietnamese. GIs make thousands of small mistakes every day that offend Vietnamese people. And the continual roaring overhead of US planes on their way to drop bombs makes people sick and angry.

So it was understandable that the villagers distrust those who are connected with the South Vietnamese government and the Americans. Along with others, I helped organize a Buddhist School of Youth for Social Service, and we have trained thousands of young people to work at community development projects in the villages. We refuse to accept money from the government or the American Military Assistance Group. We go into the villages with nothing but our own robes, and we are warmly welcomed. The peasants we work with tell us that the government officials assigned to "assist" them keep thousands of piasters a month for themselves and do nothing for them. They have come to dislike the Vietcong and fear the Americans, whose bombs continue to fall down on them.

If the US wants to escalate the war, we Vietnamese cannot stop you. Even changes of government will make no difference. The war will go on. Venerable Thich Tri Quang believes we may attain peace indirectly by means of political maneuvering and through elections. He is a man of action, courage, and intelligence, whose life is exemplary. But other Buddhists are trying to create a new

Buddhist path emphasizing ways of helping the people who live on the land. I myself doubt that much will be gained by indirect political maneuvering against the government and the Catholics, as long as the US is determined to continue the war. Underlying our struggles with the government in Da Nang and other cities is the unstated question of whether the war will go on, and this only the US can decide. I believe that the most effective thing we can do is to advocate peace, however dangerous it may be, by telling the world that we do not accept this war, that the communists are growing stronger every day they continue to be fought, and that a cease-fire must be arranged with the Vietcong as soon as possible. Then we would welcome the help of Americans in the peaceful reconstruction of our country. Only America has the capability to stop this war, which is destroying not only our lives, but our culture and everything of human value.

The poems that follow are not typical of my own poetry or of Vietnamese poetry generally. The tradition of poetry in Vietnam is very old and complex. It draws on early Chinese poetry, on the French Romantic and symbolist poets of the nineteenth and twentieth centuries, and, in my own case, on Zen Buddhist writers. Much of my poetry could be called "philosophical," and friends have found it in some ways similar to the work of Tagore; at least, it is extremely difficult to translate it into English.

But the poems published here are different. They are popular poems in free verse, and when I write them, I feel I am trying to speak very simply for the majority of Vietnamese who are peasants and cannot speak for themselves. They do not know or care much about words like "communism" or "democracy" but only want the war to end so they can survive. I wrote the poems first for myself; when I read them over, I can regain once more the state of intense feeling in which I composed them. They have now been read and heard by many Vietnamese; and they have been denounced by both sides fighting in the war. A few days after they were published last year, government police came to seize them from the bookstores, but by then they had all been sold. They were attacked by the Hanoi radio and by the radio of the National Liberation Front. They have since been read in public along with the peace poems of other Buddhists, and they have been sung with guitar accompaniment at student meetings, much as songs of protest are sung in the United States.

CONDEMNATION

Listen to this:
Yesterday six Vietcong came through my village,
and because of this, the village was bombed.
Every soul was killed.
When I returned to the village the next day,
there was nothing but clouds of dust—
the pagoda without roof or altar,
only the foundations of houses are left,
the bamboo thickets burned away.

Here in the presence of the undisturbed stars,
in the invisible presence of all people still alive on Earth,
let me raise my voice to denounce this dreadful war,
this murder of brothers by brothers!

Whoever is listening, be my witness:
I cannot accept this war.
I never could, I never will.
I must say this a thousand times before I am killed.

I am like the bird that dies for the sake of its mate,
dripping blood from its broken beak and crying out,
"Beware! Turn around to face your real enemies—
ambition, violence, hatred, greed."
Men cannot be our enemies—even men called Vietcong.
If we kill men, what brothers will we have left?
With whom shall we live then?

OUR GREEN GARDEN

Fires spring up at ten points of the universe.
A furious, acrid wind sweeps toward us from all sides.
Aloof and beautiful, the mountains and rivers abide.

All around, the horizon burns with the color of death.
As for me, yes, I am still alive,
but my body and soul writhe as if they too
had been set on fire.
My parched eyes can shed no more tears.

Where are you going this evening, dear brother,
in what direction?
The rattle of gunfire is close at hand.
In her breast, the heart of our mother
shrivels and fades
like a dying flower.
She bows her head, the smooth black hair
now threaded with white.
How many nights has she crouched wide awake,
alone with her lantern, praying for the storm to end?

Dearest brother, I know it is you who will shoot me tonight,
piercing our mother's heart with a wound
that can never heal.
O terrible winds that blow from the ends of the Earth,
hurling down our houses and blasting our fertile fields!

I say farewell to the blazing, blackening place
where I was born.
Here is my breast! Aim your gun at it, brother, shoot!
I offer my body, the body our mother bore and nurtured.
Destroy it if you wish.
Destroy it in the name of your dream—
that dream in whose name you kill.

Can you hear me invoke the darkness?
"When will these sufferings end?
O darkness, in whose name do you destroy?"

Come back, dear brother, and kneel at our mother's knee.
Don't sacrifice our green garden
to the ragged flames that are carried into the dooryard
by wild winds from far away.

Here is my breast. Aim your gun at it, brother, shoot!
Destroy me if you wish
and build from my carrion
whatever it is
you are dreaming of.

Who will be left to celebrate a victory
made of blood and fire?

PEACE

They woke me this morning
to tell me my brother had been killed in battle.
Yet in the garden,
a new rose, with moist petals uncurling,
blooms on the bush.
And I am alive,
still breathing the fragrance of roses and dung,
eating, praying, and sleeping.
When can I break my long silence?
When can I speak the unuttered words that are choking me?

FOUR

The Menton Statement

A Message to Our 3.5 Billion Neighbors on Planet Earth, 1970

Together with Alfred Hassler of the Fellowship of Reconciliation and other leading intellectuals and scientists, Thich Nhat Hanh and Sister Chan Khong helped convene Europe's first conference on the environment in Menton, France.* The conference produced this statement. Warning of the "unprecedented common danger" facing mankind, the statement was signed by 2,200 scientists from twenty-three countries and addressed to their "3.5 billion neighbors on Planet Earth." It was handed to United Nations Secretary-General U Thant at a simple ceremony in New York on May 11, 1971.†

---

* Alfred Hassler (1910–1991) was an anti-war author and activist, active during World War II and the Vietnam War. He worked with the US branch of the Fellowship of Reconciliation (FOR USA), an interfaith peace and social justice organization, from 1942 to 1974.

† In response to the Menton Statement, the Secretary-General declared: "I believe that mankind is at last aware of the fact that there is a delicate equilibrium of physical and biological phenomena on and around the earth which cannot be thoughtlessly disturbed as we race along the road of technological development. This global concern in the face of a grave common danger, which carries the seeds of extinction for the human species, may well prove to be the elusive force which can bind men together. The battle for human survival can only be won by all nations joining together in a concerted drive to preserve life on this planet."

The "Menton Message"—as it has come to be known since being drafted at a meeting in Menton, a town in southeast France—has been circulated among biologists and environmental scientists in Europe, North America, Africa, Asia, and South America. Among the signatories of the Menton Message are four Nobel Prize laureates (Salvador Luria, Jacques Monod, Albert Szent-Gyorgyi, and George Wald), and scientists Jean Rostand, Sir Julian Huxley, Thor Heyerdahl, Paul Ehrlich, Margaret Mead, René Dumont, Lord Ritchie-Calder, Shutaro Yamamoto, Gerardo Budowski, Enrique Beltran, and Mohamed Zaki Barakat.

THE MENTON STATEMENT

Widely separated though we are geographically, with very different cultures, languages, attitudes, political and religious loyalties, we are united in our time by an unprecedented common danger. This danger, of a nature and magnitude never before faced by humankind, is born of a confluence of several phenomena. Each of them would present us with almost unmanageable problems; together they present not only the probability of vast increases in human suffering in the immediate future, but the possibility of the extinction, or virtual extinction, of human life on Earth.

As biological and other environmental scientists, we do not speak to the feasibility of particular solutions to these problems, but out of our conviction that the problems exist, are global and interrelated, and that solutions can be found only if we abandon limited selfish interests to the realization of a common need.

The Problems

ENVIRONMENTAL DETERIORATION. *The quality of our environment is deteriorating at an unprecedented rate. It is more obvious in some parts of the world than in others, and in those areas public alarm has begun to express itself, while in other areas environmental deterioration seems a remote and irrelevant phenomenon.*

But there is only one environment; what happens to a part affects the whole. The most widely recognized example of this process is the penetration into food-chains all over the world of poisonous substances such as mercury, lead, cadmium, DDT, and other chlorinated organic compounds, which have been found in the tissues of birds and other animals far removed from the origin of the poisons.

Oil spills, industrial refuse, and effluents of various kinds have adversely affected nearly all fresh and inshore waters around the world, as have sewage and organic wastes released in amounts too great to be taken care of by the normal recycling processes of nature. Cities are overhung with heavy clouds of smog, and air-borne pollutants have killed trees hundreds of miles from their source.

Even more alarming are our continued and reckless ventures into new technological processes and projects (e.g., supersonic transport and the planned proliferation of nuclear power plants) without a pause to consider their possible long-term effects on the environment.

DEPLETION OF NATURAL RESOURCES. *Although Earth and its resources are finite and in part exhaustible; industrial society is using up many of its non-renewable resources and mismanaging potentially renewable ones, and it exploits the resources of other countries without regard for the deprivation of present populations or the needs of future generations.*

The Earth is already beginning to run short of some materials of critical importance to a technological society, and plans are being made to mine minerals from beneath the oceans. But such efforts not only will require vast expenditures of money and energy (and our energy-producing fuels are limited), but should not be undertaken before careful studies have been made of their probable effects on marine animal and plant life, also part of our natural resources and a source of high-protein food.

Almost all of the world's well-watered, fertile farmland is already in use. Yet each year, especially in industrialized nations, millions of acres of this land are taken out of cultivation for use as industrial sites, roads, parking lots, etc. Deforestation, damming of rivers, one-crop farming, uncontrolled use of pesticides and defoliants, strip-mining, and other short-sighted or unproductive practices have contributed to an ecological imbalance that has already had catastrophic effects in some areas and over a long term may adversely affect the productivity of large sections of the world.

Even under the best of circumstances, the Earth could not provide resources in amounts sufficient to enable all people to live at the level of consumption enjoyed by the majority in the industrial societies, and the contrast between lifestyles dictated by extreme poverty and those permitted by affluence will continue to be a source of conflict and revolution.

POPULATION, OVERCROWDING, AND HUNGER. *The present population of Earth is estimated at 3,500 million people, and calculations, based on the success of present population control programs, put it at 6,500 million by the year 2000. There have been some optimistic predictions that technological and natural resources can be developed to feed, clothe, and house far larger populations than this.*

The immediate fact is, however, that as many as two-thirds of the world's present population are suffering from malnutrition and that the threat of large-scale famine is still with us despite some nutritional advances. Pollution and ecological disruption are already affecting some food sources, and frequently, efforts to raise nutritional standards are themselves polluting.

Moreover, population figures are misleading, since they do not take into consideration the factor of consumption. It has been estimated that a child born in the United States today will consume during his lifetime at least twenty times as much as one born in India, and contribute about fifty times as much pollution to the environment. In terms of environmental impact, therefore, the most industrialized countries are also the most densely populated.

The human need for space and a degree of solitude, though difficult to state in precise terms, is real and observable. We do not live by bread alone. Even if technology could produce enough synthetic food for all, overcrowding produced by ever-rising populations is likely to have disastrous social and ecological consequences.

WAR. *Throughout history there has been no human activity so universally condemned and so universally practiced as war, and research on ever more destructive weaponry and methods of warfare has been unremitting.*

Now that we have achieved the ultimate weapon and seen its potential, we have recoiled from its further use, but our fear has not kept us from filling our arsenals with enough nuclear warheads to wipe out all life on earth several times over, or from blind and heedless experiments, both in the laboratory and in the battlefield, with biological and chemical weapons. Nor has it kept us from engaging in "small" wars or aggressive actions that may lead to nuclear war.

Even if a final, major war is avoided, preparation for it uses up physical and human resources that ought to be spent in an effort to find ways of feeding and housing the world's deprived people and of saving and improving the environment.

It is clear that it is insufficient to attribute war to the natural belligerence of humankind when we have in fact succeeded in establishing at some points stable and relatively peaceful societies in limited geographical areas. In our time it is apparent that the dangers of global war focus at two points:

- the inequality that exists between industrialized and non-industrialized parts of the world and the determination of millions of impoverished human beings to improve their lot;

- the competition for power and economic advantage among anarchic nation-states unwilling to relinquish selfish interests in order to create a more equitable society.

Stated thus, the problem seems almost insoluble. Yet humankind has demonstrated improbable resources of adaptability and resilience in the past and perhaps facing what may well be the ultimate challenge to its survival, it will confound our fears once again.

What can be done?

The preceding is only a partial listing of the problems that confront us and makes scarcely any attempt to describe their causes. We really do not know the full dimensions of either our problems or their solutions. We do know that Earth and all of its inhabitants are in trouble and that our problems will multiply if we do not attend to them.

In the 1940s, when it was decided to develop the atomic bomb, the United States appropriated 2,000 million dollars and brought experts from all over the world to do the job in two years. In the 1960s, preoccupied with the race to the moon, the United States spent between 20,000 and 40,000 million dollars to win the race, and both the Soviet Union and the US continue to spend thousands of millions of dollars in space exploration.

Certainly, massive research into the problems that threaten the survival of humankind deserves a higher priority than atomic or space research. It should be begun at once on a similar scale and with an even greater sense of urgency. Such research should be paid for by the industrial nations, which are not only financially best able to carry that burden, but are themselves the principal users of resources and the major polluters. The research should be carried out by qualified people from all countries and various professions, unfettered by restrictive nationalistic policies.

Because the crisis is so pressing, however, we urge that the following actions be taken even while research is going on. We do not offer these as panaceas, but as holding actions to keep our situation from deteriorating past the point of no return:

- A moratorium on technological innovations the effects of which we cannot foretell and which are not essential to human survival. This would include new weapons systems, luxury transport, new and untested pesticides, the manufacture of new plastics, the establishment of vast new nuclear power projects, etc. It would also include ecologically unresearched engineering projects, the damming of great rivers, "reclamation" of jungle land, undersea mining projects, etc.

- The application of existing pollution-control technology to the generation of energy and to industry generally, large scale recycling of materials in order to slow down the exhaustion of resources, and the rapid establishment of international agreements on environmental quality, subject to review as environmental needs become more fully known.

- Intensified programs in all regions of the world to curb population growth, with full regard for the necessity of accomplishing this without abrogation of civil rights. It is important that these programs be accompanied by a decrease in the level of consumption by privileged classes, and that a more equitable distribution of food and other goods among all people be developed.

- Regardless of the difficulty of achieving agreements, nations must find a way to abolish war, to defuse their nuclear armaments, and to destroy their chemical and biological weapons. The consequences of a global war would be immediate and irreversible, and it is therefore also the responsibility of individuals and groups to refuse to participate in research or processes that might, if used, result in the extermination of the human species.

Earth, which has seemed so large, must now be seen in its smallness. We live in a closed system, absolutely dependent on Earth and on each other for our lives and those of succeeding generations. The many things that divide us are therefore of infinitely lesser importance than the interdependence and danger that unite us.

We believe that it is literally true that only by transcending our divisions will we be able to keep Earth as our home. Solutions to the actual problems of pollution, hunger, overpopulation and war may be simpler to find than the formula for the common effort through which the search for solutions must occur, but we must make a beginning.

FIVE

From Weapons to Human Solidarity, 1971

This essay was adapted for the first edition of *Love in Action* from a speech Thich Nhat Hanh gave in the United States in 1971, still four years before the end of the war in Vietnam.

All things are interconnected. The nuclear arms race is inextricably linked to other forms of violence and suffering that afflict life on Earth. Recognizing this, I propose reductions in military spending with corresponding allocations to be used for the alleviation of world hunger. As the strongest nation on Earth, the United States can take the first step with an independent initiative for stopping the arms race, and this action can be taken regardless of the actions that are taken or not taken by any other country. Let the money that is saved by reductions in defense spending be spent for jobs and industries that grow, process, and ship food to the starving children of the world.

I address this proposal to the people of the United States, and in particular to my colleagues in the religious and peace communities. Forty thousand children a day and ten million people a year die of starvation. This suffering cannot be alleviated by government action alone. As individuals, we must also assume responsibility and lend our efforts and our hearts to the work of ending human suffering and building human solidarity. For example, if people in Western countries reduced their consumption of meat and alcohol by just 50 percent, the resultant availability of grain would change the fate of millions of starving people in the developing countries.

During the war in Vietnam, we proposed a cease-fire plan to the Americans. It was the voice of those who were being bombed. The proposal was for the Americans to independently declare a cease-fire and then invite the other side to respond, promising that if the other responded, the US would set a timetable for total withdrawal from Vietnam. The same can be done regarding the manufacture of arms.

I hope the United States will independently declare a stop to the arms race and invite Russia, China, and all other arms-producing countries to do the same. This could be done for six months, with or without reciprocation. Then, if other countries do reciprocate, the US could take another step toward complete and general disarmament. In this way, through varying stages, defense spending could be reduced while at the same time resources could be redirected to alleviate human suffering.

This proposal is offered for the endorsement of all religious denominations, international peace organizations, and other people and organizations that share in the common cause of disarmament and development. I strongly urge these friends to work to create jobs that nurture the peace and well-being of humanity in order to offer alternative employment to those engaged in the manufacture and sale of the weapons that, even at this moment, are destroying lives of people all over the world.

SIX

On Simplicity, 1975

"On Simplicity" was originally printed in Fellowship of Reconciliation's *Fellowship Magazine* in March 1975 as "The Montagnards' Way of Simplicity." *Montagnard* is a French word that means "mountain dweller," and refers to the indigenous peoples of the Central Highlands of Vietnam, not far from Thich Nhat Hanh's birthplace in Hue.

In 1951, I went with a few fellow monks to a remote mountain in the Dai Lao region of Vietnam to build a hermitage.* We asked some native mountain people for their help, and two Montagnards from the Jarai tribe joined us in clearing the forest, cutting trees into lumber, and gathering other materials for construction. They were hard workers, and we were grateful for their assistance. But after working with us for only three days, they stopped coming. Without their help, we had many difficulties, as we were not familiar with the ways of the forest. So we walked to their village and asked what had happened. They said, "Why should we return so soon? You already

---

* Learn more about Thich Nhat Hanh's experience in this small, isolated hermitage (named Phuong Boi) in *Fragrant Palm Leaves* (Parallax Press, 2020).

paid us enough to live for a month! We will come again when we run out of rice." At the time, it was a common practice to underpay the Montagnards, to avoid just this kind of thing. We had paid them properly, and, sure enough, they stopped coming.

Many people criticized the Montagnards for this ethic. They said that this laziness could only lead to trouble, and they listed four reasons to support their claim: (1) The Montagnards would be happier and more comfortable if they worked harder. (2) They would earn more money, which they could save for difficult periods. (3) The Montagnards should work harder in order to help others. (4) If they worked harder, they would have the means to defend themselves from invasions and exploitation. There may be some validity to each of these points, but if we look closely at the lives of the Montagnards, we will come to understand them, and ourselves, better.

1. The Montagnards would be happier and more comfortable if they worked harder.

The Montagnards lived simply. They did not store much food at all. They had no bank accounts. But they were much more serene and at peace with themselves, nature, and other people than almost anyone in the world. I am not suggesting that we all return to primitive lifestyles, but it is important that we see and appreciate the wisdom in a lifestyle like this, a wisdom that those of us immersed in modernization and economic growth have lost.

How much stuff do we need to be happy and comfortable? Happiness and comfort vary according to taste. Some people think they need three or four houses—one on the Riviera, one in New York, one in Tokyo, and perhaps one in Fiji. Others find that a two- or three-room hut is quite enough. In fact, if you own a dozen luxurious houses, you may rarely have time to enjoy them. Even when you have the time, you may not know how to sit peacefully in one place. Always seeking distraction—going to restaurants, the theater, or dinner parties, or taking vacations that exhaust you even more—you can't stand being alone and facing yourself directly.

In former times, people spent hours drinking one cup of tea with dear friends. A cup of tea does not cost much, but today, we go to a café and take less than five minutes to drink our tea or coffee, and even during that short time, we are mostly thinking and talking about other things, and we never even notice our tea. Even those of us who own just one house barely have the time to live in it. We leave home early in the morning after a quick breakfast and go off to work, spending an hour in the car or the train and the rest of the day in the office. Then we return home exhausted, eat dinner, watch TV, and collapse so we can get up early for work. Is this "progress"?

The Montagnards were quite content to live in simple bamboo and palm-leaf huts and wash their clothes by hand. They refused to be slaves to economic pressures. Content with just a few possessions, they rarely needed to spend their time or money seeing doctors or psychotherapists for stress-related ailments.

2. *They would earn more money, which they could save for difficult periods.*

How much do we need to save? We do not save air because we trust that it will be available to us when we need it. Why must we stockpile food, money, or other things for our own private use while so many others are hungry?

People who accumulate a house, a car, a position, and so forth, identify themselves with what they own, and they think that if they lose their house, their car, or their position, they would not be themselves. To me, they are already lost. By accumulating and saving, they have constructed a false self, and in the process they have forgotten their truest and deepest self. Psychotherapists can try to help, but the cause of this illness lies in their way of life. One way to help such a person would be to place them in an "underdeveloped" country where they could grow their own food and make their own clothes. Sharing the fate and simple life of peasants might help them heal quickly.

We have enough resources and know-how to assure every human being of adequate shelter and food every day. If we don't help others live, we ourselves are not going to be able to live either. We are all in the same boat—planet Earth. Why not put our efforts into trying to help each other and save our boat instead of accumulating savings only for ourselves and our own children?

3. *The Montagnards should work harder in order to help others.*

Of course, the Montagnards could have spent more time working in order to send aid to people who were starving in other parts of the world. If they did not do so, it was because they didn't know much about the existence of other nations. They certainly did help their own tribal members whenever they got sick or when a crop was destroyed by some natural disaster. But let us reflect for a moment on what the Montagnard people did *not* do.

They did not harm or exploit others. They grew their own food and exchanged some of their products with other people. They did not do violence to nature. They cut only enough wood to build their houses. They cleared only enough land to plant their crops.

Because of their simple lifestyle, they did not over consume natural resources. They did not pollute the air, water, or soil. They used very little fuel and no electricity. They did not own private cars, dishwashers, or electric razors. The way they lived enabled natural resources to continually renew themselves. A lifestyle like theirs demonstrates that a future for humankind is possible, and this is the most helpful thing anyone can do for others.

4. If they worked harder, they would have the means to defend themselves from invasion and exploitation.

It is true that the Montagnards were exploited by others and were often victims of social injustice. They lived in remote mountain areas. If others settled nearby, they risked losing their land due to a lack of means with which to defend themselves.

People said that if the rest of us in Vietnam worked as little as they did, our country would never be able to resist foreign intervention and exploitation. It seems clear that the Montagnards and others like them had to do something more. But what? If the Montagnards had moved down to the more populated areas, they would have seen men and women working terribly hard and getting poorer. They would have seen how expensive food, lodging, electricity, water, clothing, and transportation were. Their civilized countrymen were working all day long and could barely pay for the most basic items they consumed. The Montagnards in the forest did not need to spend any money. If they had lived and worked in the cities, how would that have helped Vietnam resist foreign intervention? All they would have learned is that in the so-called developed nations, resources are used to make bombs and other elaborate weapons, while many citizens live in misery. The Montagnards might well need nuclear weapons to resist foreign intervention if they were to catch up with their more "developed" brothers and sisters. Will social injustice ever be abolished before all people wake up and realize that unless we let others live, we ourselves will not be able to live?

Economic growth may be necessary for the welfare of people, but the present rate of economic growth is destroying humanity and nature. Injustice is rampant. We humans are part of nature, and harming nature only harms ourselves. It is not just the poor and oppressed who are victims of environmental damage. The affluent are just as much victims of pollution and the exploitation of resources. We must look at the whole picture and ask, "Does our way of life harm nature? Does our way of life harm our fellow humans? Do we live at the expense of others, at the expense of the present, and at the expense of the future?" If we answer truthfully, we will know how to orient our lives and our actions. We have much to learn from the Montagnards and others like them. We must learn to live in a way that makes a future possible.

SEVEN

The Human Family, 1975

"The Human Family" was adapted from a talk entitled "Man and Nature" that was given to psychiatrists at the World Federation of Mental Health World Congress in Copenhagen, August 1975.

Although human beings are a part of nature, we single ourselves out and classify other animals and living beings as "nature," while acting as if we were somehow separate from it. Then we ask, "How should we deal with nature?" We should deal with nature the way we should deal with ourselves! Nonviolently. We should not harm ourselves, and we should not harm nature. To harm nature is to harm ourselves, and vice versa. If we knew how to deal with ourselves and our fellow human beings, we would know how to deal with nature. Human beings and nature are inseparable. By not caring properly for either, we harm both.

We can only be happy when we accept ourselves as we are. We must first be aware of all the elements within us, and then we must bring them into harmony. Our physical and mental well-being are the result of understanding what is going on in ourselves. This understanding helps us respect nature in ourselves and also helps us bring about healing.

If we harm another human being, we harm ourselves. To accumulate wealth and own excessive portions of the world's natural resources is to deprive our fellow humans of the chance to live. To participate in oppressive and unjust social systems is to widen the gap between rich and poor and thereby aggravate the situation of social injustice. Yet we tolerate excess, injustice, and war while remaining unaware that the human race as a family is suffering. While some members of the human family are suffering and starving, for us to enjoy false security and wealth is a sign of insanity.

The fate of each individual is inextricably linked to the fate of the whole human race. We must let others live if we ourselves want to live. The only alternative to coexistence is co-nonexistence. A civilization in which we kill and exploit others for our own aggrandizement is sick. For us to have a healthy civilization, everyone must be born with an equal right to education, work, food, shelter, world citizenship, and the ability to circulate freely and settle on any part of the Earth. Political and economic systems that deny one person these rights harm the whole human family. We must begin by becoming aware of what is happening to every member of the human family if we want to repair the damage already done.

To bring about peace, we must work for harmonious coexistence. If we continue to shut ourselves off from the rest of the world, imprisoning ourselves in our narrow concerns and immediate problems, we are not likely to make peace or to survive. It is difficult for one individual to preserve harmony among the elements within themselves, and it is even more difficult to preserve harmony among the members of the human family. We have to understand the human race to bring it into harmony. Cruelty and disruption destroy the harmony of the family. We need legislation that keeps us from doing violence to ourselves or nature and prevents us from being disruptive and cruel.

We have created a system that we cannot control. This system imposes itself on us, and we have become its slaves. Most of us, in order to have a house, a car, a refrigerator, a TV, and so on, must sacrifice our time and our lives in exchange. We are constantly under the pressure of time. In former times, we could afford three hours for one cup of tea, enjoying the company of our friends in a serene and spiritual atmosphere. We could organize a party to celebrate the blossoming of one orchid in our garden. But today we can no longer afford these things. We say that time is money. We have created a society in which the rich become richer, and the poor become poorer. We are so caught up in our own immediate problems that we cannot afford to be aware of what is going on with the rest of the human family. We see images on TV, but we do not really understand our Third World brothers and sisters.

The individual and all of humanity are both part of nature and should be able to live in harmony with nature. Nature can be cruel and disruptive and therefore, at times, needs to be controlled. To control is not to dominate or oppress but to harmonize and equilibrate. We must be deep friends with nature in order to control certain aspects of it. This requires a full understanding of nature. Typhoons, tornadoes, droughts, floods, volcanic eruptions, and proliferations of harmful insects all constitute danger and destruction to life. Although natural, these things disrupt nature's harmony. We should be able to prevent to a large degree the destruction that natural disasters cause, but we must do it in a way that preserves life and encourages harmony.

The excessive use of pesticides that kill all kinds of insects and upset the ecological balance is an example of our lack of wisdom in trying to control nature. Economic growth that devastates nature by polluting and exhausting nonrenewable resources, rendering the Earth impossible for beings to live on, is another. Such economic growth may appear to benefit some humans, but in reality it disrupts and destroys the whole of nature to which we all belong.

The harmony and equilibrium in the individual, society, and nature are being destroyed. Individuals are sick, society is sick, and nature is sick. We must reestablish harmony and equilibrium, but how? Where can we begin the work of healing? Would we begin with the individual, society, or the environment? We must work in all three domains. People of different disciplines tend to stress their particular areas. For example, politicians consider an effective rearrangement of society necessary for the salvation of humans and nature, and therefore urge that everyone engage in the struggle to change political systems.

We Buddhist monks are like psychotherapists in that we tend to look at the problem from the viewpoint of mental health. Meditation aims at creating harmony and equilibrium in the life of the individual. Buddhist meditation uses the breath as a tool to calm and harmonize the whole human being. As in any therapeutic practice, the patient is placed in an environment that favors the restoration of harmony. Usually, psychotherapists spend their time observing and then advising their patients. I know of some, however, who, like monks, observe themselves first, recognizing the need to free their own selves from the fears, anxieties, and despair that exist in each of us. Many therapists seem to think that they themselves have no mental problems, but the monk recognizes in himself the susceptibility to fears and anxieties, and to the mental illness that is caused by the inhuman social and economic systems that prevail in today's world.

Buddhists believe that the reality of the individual, society, and nature's integral being will reveal itself to us as we recover, gradually ceasing to be possessed by anxiety, fear, and the dispersion of mind. Among the three—individual, society, and nature—it is the individual who begins to effect change. But in order to effect change, the individual must have personally recovered, must be whole. Since this requires an environment favorable to healing, we must seek the kind of lifestyle that is free from destructiveness. Efforts to change the environment and to change the individual are both necessary, but it is difficult to change the environment if individuals are not in a state of equilibrium. From the mental health point of view, efforts to recover our humanness should be given priority.

Restoring mental health does not mean simply helping individuals adjust to the modern world of rapid economic growth. The world is sick: adapting to an unwell environment will not bring real health. Many people who seek the help of a psychotherapist are really victims of modern life which separates human beings from the rest of nature. One way to help such a person may be to move them to a rural area where they can cultivate the land, grow their own food, wash their clothes in a clear river, and live simply, sharing the same life as millions of peasants around the world.

For psychotherapy to be effective, we need environmental change, and psychotherapists must participate in efforts to change the environment. But that is only half their task. The other half is to help individuals be themselves, not by helping them adapt to an ill environment, but by providing them with the strength to change it. To tranquilize them is not the way. The explosion of bombs, the burning of napalm, the violent deaths of relatives and neighbors, the pressures of time, noise, and pollution, the lonely crowds—these have all been created by the disruptive course of our economic growth. They are all sources of mental illness, and they must end. Anything we can do to bring them to an end is preventive medicine. Political activities are not the only means to this end.

While helping their particular patients, psychotherapists must, at the same time, recognize their responsibility to the whole human family. Their work must also prevent others from becoming ill. They are challenged to safeguard their own humanness. Like others, psychotherapists and monastics first need to observe themselves and their own way of life. If they do, I believe they will seek ways to disengage themselves from the present economic systems in order to help reestablish harmony and balance in life. Monastics and psychotherapists are human beings. We cannot escape mental illness if we do not apply our disciplines to ourselves. Caught in forgetfulness and acquiescence to the status quo, we will gradually become victims of fear, anxiety, and egotism of all kinds. But if psychotherapists and monastics, through mutual sharing, help each other apply our disciplines to our own lives, we will rediscover the harmony in ourselves and thereby help the whole human family.

A tree reveals itself to an artist when the artist can establish a genuine relationship with it. If a human is not a real human being, they may look at their fellow humans and not see them; they may look at a tree and not see it. Many of us cannot see things because we are not wholly ourselves. When we are wholly ourselves, we can see how one person, by living fully, demonstrates to all of us that life is possible, that a future is possible. But the question "Is a future possible?" is meaningless without seeing the millions of our fellow humans who suffer, live, and die around us. Only when we really see them will we be able to see ourselves and see nature.

EIGHT

I Have Lost My Brother, 1982

"I Have Lost My Brother" is from a public talk given at the interfaith Reverence for Life Conference in New York on June 9, 1982, in connection with the opening of the United Nations's second special session on disarmament. The conference was sponsored by the Temple of Understanding, an educational agency with headquarters in New York founded to enlist the spiritual resources of all religions in building a better world, drawing on inspiration from such figures as Albert Schweitzer, Mahatma Gandhi, and Thomas Merton.

Several autumns ago, I walked up to the pine tree in my backyard and asked it one question: "What is institutional violence?" The tree did not answer right away. So, I sat at its roots and waited. The backyard was covered with brilliantly colored leaves, the air was fresh, and suddenly I forgot that I was waiting for an answer. The tree and I were just there, enjoying ourselves and each other. After sitting for a long time, I turned to the tree, smiled, and said, "I no longer need an answer." Then I thanked it and awarded it the Grand Transnational Peace Prize.

When I told my friends this, one asked, "Do you give the Peace Prize often?" I did not know how to answer. I wanted to, but it was difficult. Then another asked, "What was the tree's answer to your question?" Again, I did not know what to say, so I encouraged her to go out and ask the tree.

As a novice monk, I was taught to look deeply at a cypress tree, and I learned that looking at a cypress can be very helpful. In fact, it is often easier to contemplate a cypress than to talk to a person. Before talking to a human being, watching a cypress can help. Soon I will organize an International Conference on Tree Watching. All of the conferees will sit in the forest and just look at beautiful cypresses and pines. Then, in workshops, we can discuss strategies for tree watching and also principles for appreciating human beings, even those who do not look or think exactly as we do. When I told this to the pine tree, it began to laugh. The tree was thinking about a particular conference held at a Hilton Hotel dealing with the problems of the "Third World." Not a single Third World representative had the opportunity to speak because eloquent spokespersons from the First World spoke for them. It was too difficult for them to listen to real Third World representatives, especially those whose ideas did not fit in with their own.

—

I have lost my brother and I don't know where and how to find him. My brother was accused of destroying the community because he wanted to do things differently. Now the community continues, but my brother is missing. I have been on a pilgrimage for years looking for him, but without your help, I will never succeed.

Yesterday, I stood in a park and watched a three-year-old child with all my attention, and I was heartbroken. When people say, "Things aren't too bad," I am not sure they understand. If we continue to live the way we do, what kind of world are we leaving for our children? Are we leaving any world at all?

I know my brother is still alive, and I will travel all over the world to find him. But I really need your help. Will you help me? He may be hard to recognize, but I believe the time is near. When the rest of us were asleep, my brother saw what was happening. He tried to tell us, but we never listened. We were busy doing other things—practicing meditation, praying, reciting scriptures. We were not at all awake.

People thought my brother was dangerous, but it is not true. He is outspoken, but not dangerous. In fact, not listening to him is what is dangerous. One person like my brother counts for a lot. When I think of him, I know that peace is possible. Please help me find him. If we succeed, there will be hope.

If we try to remove the bombs from a distance, we can never succeed. The bombs are us, and my brother understands that. He asked why we export conventional weapons to the poorest countries of the Third World while people there are starving. I am not trying to make you sad. I just want to share some of the things my brother said.

When I look at the three-year-old child, when I look at the pine tree, I feel co-responsible for their futures. I have no money and no weapons, but I know that by not being attentive enough, I have allowed the situation to develop this far. We are all much too busy. If my brother returns home soon, we will have a chance. That is what I feel. But I am not sure all of us will be able to listen to him or understand him. We only have a chance if we are able to hear and truly understand him. If we are, we may be willing to change our ways. We still do not know how to take care of him. So, we have to prepare. We have to look deeply into our daily lives, at the ways we think and act, and begin to live in a way that allows the return of my brother to be possible, that allows a future to be possible.

My brother said, "Each person is important. Each being is important. Each moment is important." I am sure the pine tree and the three-year-old child understand this. Our opportunity for peace is not later. It is now. My brother was considered too dangerous for the material well-being of the community. He was a little too radical, too outspoken. That is why we did not want him. But I can assure you that one person like my brother counts for a lot. I have confidence in my brother now, because as I think of him, I feel that anything is possible. Please help. Please be attentive. If you are attentive enough, you will find my brother. Please do not leave me in distress. Tell me, write me, telephone me the moment you see him. I know it may be hard to recognize him, but he is around. He may be living in a monastery, or he may be somewhere on the street or in the marketplace. Or he may be within your own heart.

NINE

Call Me by My True Names, 1983

In sharing his thoughts about the writing of his 1976 poem, "Call Me by My True Names"—probably the most famous of all of his poems—at a public talk given in May 1983 at the Rochester Zen Center in Rochester, New York, Thich Nhat Hanh offered profound teachings on not taking sides and the awareness that leads to the possibility of peace with our enemies.

In 1976, I wrote a poem about a twelve-year-old girl, one of the boat people crossing the Gulf of Siam, who was raped by a sea pirate and threw herself into the sea; the pirate, who was born in a remote village along the coast in Thailand; and me. I was not on the boat—in fact, I was thousands of miles away—but because I was mindful, I knew what was going on in the Gulf.

I was angry when I received the news of her death, but I learned after meditating for several hours that I could not just take sides against the pirate. I saw that if I had been born in his village and brought up under the same conditions, I would be exactly like him. Taking sides is too easy. Out of my suffering, I wrote this poem, entitled "Please Call Me by My True Names." I have many names, and when you call me by any of them, I have to say, "Yes."

> Don't say that I will depart tomorrow—
> even today I am still arriving.
>
> Look deeply: every second I am arriving
> to be a bud on a spring branch,
> to be a tiny bird, with still-fragile wings,
> learning to sing in my new nest,
> to be a caterpillar in the heart of a flower,
> to be a jewel hiding itself in a stone.
>
> I still arrive, in order to laugh and to cry,
> to fear and to hope.
>
> The rhythm of my heart is the birth and death
> of all that is alive.
>
> I am the mayfly metamorphosing
> on the surface of the river.
> And I am the bird,
> that swoops down to swallow the mayfly.
>
> I am the frog swimming happily
> in the clear water of a pond.
> And I am the grass-snake
> that silently feeds itself on the frog.
>
> I am the child in Uganda, all skin and bones,
> my legs as thin as bamboo sticks.
> And I am the arms merchant,
> selling deadly weapons to Uganda.

I am the twelve-year-old girl,
refugee on a small boat,
who throws herself into the ocean
after being raped by a sea pirate.
And I am the pirate,
my heart not yet capable
of seeing and loving.

I am a member of the politburo,
with plenty of power in my hands.
And I am the man who has to pay
his "debt of blood" to my people,
dying slowly in a forced-labor camp.

My joy is like spring, so warm
it makes flowers bloom all over the Earth.
My pain is like a river of tears,
so vast it fills the four oceans.

Please call me by my true names,
so I can hear all my cries and laughter at once,
so I can see that my joy and pain are one.

Please call me by my true names,
so I can wake up
and so the door of my heart,
can be left open,
the door of compassion.

We think we need an enemy. Governments work hard to get us to be afraid and to hate so we will rally behind them. If we do not have a real enemy, they will invent one in order to mobilize us. Recently I went to Russia with some American and European friends, and we found that the Russian people are wonderful. For so many years the American government told their people that Russia was "an evil empire."

It is not correct to believe that the world's situation is in the hands of the government and that if the president only had the correct policies, there would be peace. Our daily lives have the most to do with the situation of the world. If we can change our daily lives, we can change our governments, and we can change the world. Our presidents and our governments are us. They reflect our lifestyle and our way of thinking. The way we hold a cup of tea, pick up a newspaper, and even use toilet paper have to do with peace.

As a novice in a Buddhist monastery, I was taught to be aware of each thing I did throughout the day, and for more than fifty years, I have been practicing this. When I started, I thought this kind of practice was only for beginners, that advanced people did more important things, but now I know that the practice of mindfulness is for everyone. Meditation is to see into our own nature and wake up. If we are not aware of what is going on in ourselves and in the world, how can we see into our own nature and wake up? Are we really awake when we drink our tea, read our newspaper, or use the toilet?

Our society makes it difficult for us to be awake. There are so many distractions. We know that forty thousand children in the Third World die of hunger every day, but we keep forgetting. Our society makes us forgetful. That is why we need practice to help us be mindful. I know a number of friends who refrain from eating dinner two times each week in order to remember the situation in the Third World.

One day I asked a young Vietnamese refugee who was eating a bowl of rice whether children in his country eat rice of such high quality. He said no because he knows the situation. He experienced hunger in Vietnam—there were times when he ate only dried potatoes while he longed for a bowl of rice. In France, he has been eating rice for a year, and he is already beginning to forget. But when I asked him, he remembered. I could not ask the same question to a French or American child because they have not had the experience of hunger. It is difficult for people in the West to understand the situation in the Third World. It seems to have nothing to do with their situation. I told the Vietnamese boy that the rice he was eating in France came from Thailand and that most Thai children do not have rice of such high quality because the best rice is set aside for export to Japan and the West in exchange for foreign currency.

In Vietnam we have a delicious banana called *chuôi già*, but the children and adults in Vietnam do not have the right to eat these bananas because they are all for export. In return, Vietnam gets guns in order to kill ourselves and our brothers. Some of us practice this exercise of mindfulness: we sponsor a child in the Third World and get news from him or her, thus keeping in touch with the reality outside. We try many ways to be awake, but our society still keeps us forgetful. Meditation is to help us remember.

There are other ways to nourish awareness. One thirteen-year-old Dutch boy visited our retreat center and joined us for a silent lunch. It was the first time he had eaten in silence, and he was embarrassed. Afterwards, I asked him if he had felt uncomfortable, and he said yes. I explained that the reason we eat in silence is to be in touch with the food and the presence of each other. If we talk a lot, we cannot enjoy these things. I asked him if there was some time when he turned off the TV in order to enjoy his dinner more, and he said yes. Later in the day, I invited him to join us for another silent meal, and he enjoyed it very much. Society bombards us with so many noises that we have lost our taste for silence. Every time we have a few minutes, we turn on the TV or make a phone call. We do not know how to be ourselves without something to distract us. So, the first thing we need to do is to return to ourselves and reorganize our daily lives so that we are not just victims of society and other people.

To educate people for peace, we can use words, or we can speak with our lives. If we are not peaceful, if we are not feeling well in our skin, we cannot demonstrate real peace, and we cannot raise our children well either. To take good care of our children means to take good care of ourselves, to be aware of our situation. Please sit down with your child and, together, contemplate the little flowers that grow among the grasses. Breathing in and out, smiling together— that is real peace education. When we can learn to appreciate these small, beautiful things, we will not have to search for anything else. We can be peace ourselves, and we can make peace with our friends and even with our so-called enemies.

TEN

Ahimsa: The Path of Harmlessness, 1988

"Ahimsa: The Path of Harmlessness" is from two public talks given at Plum Village, France in August of 1988.

The Sanskrit word *ahimsa*, usually translated as "nonviolence," literally means "non-harming" or "harmlessness." To practice ahimsa, we first have to practice it within ourselves. In each of us, there is a certain amount of violence and a certain amount of nonviolence. Depending on our state of being, our response to things will be more or less nonviolent. Even if we take pride in being vegetarian, for example, we have to acknowledge that the water in which we boil our vegetables contains many tiny microorganisms. We cannot be completely nonviolent, but by being vegetarian, we are going in the direction of nonviolence. If we want to head north, we can use the North Star to guide us, but it is impossible to arrive at the North Star. Our effort is only to proceed in that direction.

Anyone can practice some nonviolence, even soldiers. Some generals, for example, conduct their operations in ways that avoid killing innocent people. This is a kind of nonviolence. To help other soldiers move in the nonviolent direction, we have to be in touch with them. If we divide reality into two camps—the violent and the nonviolent—and stand in one camp while attacking the other, the world will never have peace. We will always blame and condemn those we feel are responsible for wars and social injustice, without recognizing the degree of violence in ourselves. We must work on ourselves and also work with those we condemn if we want to have a real impact.

It never helps to draw a line and dismiss some people as enemies, even those who act violently. We have to approach them with love in our hearts and do our best to help them move in the direction of nonviolence. If we work for peace out of our own anger, we will never succeed. Peace is not an end. It can never come about through non-peaceful means.

When we protest against a war, we assume that we are a peaceful person, a representative of peace, but this may not be the case. If we look deeply, we may observe that the roots of war are in the unmindful ways we have been living. We have not sown enough seeds of peace and understanding in ourselves and others, so we are co-responsible: "Because I have been like this, they are like that." A more holistic approach is the way of "interbeing": "This is like this because that is like that." This is the way of understanding and love. With this kind of insight, you can see clearly and help our government see clearly. Then we can go to a demonstration and say, "This war is unjust, destructive, and not worthy of our great nation." This is far more effective than angrily condemning others. Anger always accelerates the damage.

We know how to write strong letters of protest, but we must also learn to write love letters to our president and representatives, demonstrating the kind of understanding and using the kind of language they will appreciate. If we don't, our letters may end up in the trash and help no one. To love is to understand. We cannot express love to someone unless we understand them. If we do not understand our president or congressperson, we cannot write them a love letter.

People are happy to read a good letter in which we share our insights and our understanding. When they receive that kind of letter, they will feel understood, and they will pay attention to your recommendations. You may think that the way to change the world is to elect a new president, but a government is only a reflection of society, which is a reflection of our own consciousness. To create fundamental change, we, the members of society, have to transform ourselves. If we want real peace, we have to demonstrate our love and understanding so that those responsible for making decisions can learn from us.

All of us, even pacifists, have pain inside. We feel angry and frustrated, and we need to find someone willing to listen to us who is capable of understanding our suffering. In Buddhist iconography, there is a bodhisattva named Avalokitesvara who has one thousand arms and one thousand hands and has an eye in the palm of each hand. One thousand hands represent action, and the eye in each hand represents understanding. When you understand a situation or a person, any action you do will help and not cause more suffering. When you have an eye in your hand, you know how to practice true nonviolence.

Imagine if each of our words also had an eye in it. It is easy to depict a hand with an eye, but how might an artist put an eye into our words? Before we say something, we have to understand what we are saying and also the person to whom our words are directed.

With the eye of understanding, we will not say things to make the other person suffer. Blaming and arguing are forms of violence. If we suffer greatly, our words may be bitter, and that will not help anyone. We have to learn to calm ourselves and become a flower before we speak. This is the art of loving speech.

Listening is also a deep practice. The bodhisattva Avalokitesvara has a deep talent for listening. In Chinese, his name means "listening to the cries of the world." We have to listen in a way that we understand the suffering of others. We have to empty ourselves and leave space so we can listen well. If we breathe in and out to refresh and empty ourselves, we will be able to sit still and listen. People who are suffering need someone to listen attentively without judging or reacting. If they cannot find someone in their family, they may go to a psychotherapist. Just by listening deeply, we already alleviate a great deal of their pain. This is an important practice of peace. We have to listen to our families and our communities. We have to listen to everyone, especially those we consider our enemies. When we show our capacity of listening and understanding, the other person will also listen to us, and we will have a chance to tell them of our pain. This is the beginning of healing.

Thinking is at the base of everything. It is important for us to put an eye of awareness into each of our thoughts. Without a correct understanding of a situation or a person, our thoughts can be misleading and create confusion, despair, anger, or hatred. Our most important task is to develop correct insight. If we see deeply into the nature of interbeing, that all things inter-are, we will stop blaming, arguing, and killing, and we will become friends with everyone.

These are the three domains of action—body, speech, and mind. In addition, there is non-action, which is often more important than action. Without our doing anything, things sometimes go more smoothly just because of our peaceful presence. In a small boat when a storm comes, if one person remains solid and calm, others will not panic, and the boat is more likely to stay afloat. In many circumstances, non-action can help a lot. A tree merely breathes, waves its leaves and branches, and tries to stay fresh. But if the tree were not there, we could not be here. The tree's non-action is fundamental to our well-being. If we can learn to live the way a tree does—staying fresh and solid, peaceful and calm—even if we do not do many things, others will benefit from our non-action, our presence. We can also practice non-action in the domain of speech. Words can create understanding and mutual acceptance, or they can cause others to suffer. Sometimes it is best not to say anything. This is a book on nonviolent social action, but we must also discuss nonviolent non-action. If we really want to help the world, the practice of non-action is essential.

Of course, sometimes non-action can be harmful. When someone needs our action and we refuse, they may die. If a monk, for example, sees a woman drowning and does not want to touch her because of his precepts, he will violate the most fundamental principle of life. When we see social injustice, if we practice non-action, we may cause harm. When people need us to say or do something, our inaction or our silence can kill.

To practice ahimsa, we must first learn ways to deal peacefully with ourselves. If we create true harmony within ourselves, we will know how to deal with our families, friends, and associates. Techniques are always secondary. Most important is to *become* ahimsa so that when a situation presents itself, we will not create more suffering. To practice ahimsa, we need gentleness, loving kindness, compassion, joy, and equanimity directed to our bodies, our feelings, and other people.

Real peace must be based on insight and understanding, and for this we must practice deep reflection—looking deeply into each act and each thought of our daily lives.

With mindfulness—the practice of peace—we can begin by working to transform the wars in ourselves. There are techniques for doing this. Conscious breathing is one. Every time we feel upset, we can stop what we are doing, refrain from saying anything, and breathe in and out several times, aware of each in-breath and each out-breath. If we are still upset, we can go for walking meditation, mindful of each slow step and each breath we take. By cultivating peace within, we bring about peace in society. It depends on us. To practice peace in ourselves is to minimize the number of wars between this-or-that feeling, or this-or-that perception, and we can then have real peace with others as well, including the members of our own family.

I am often asked, "What if you are practicing love and patience and someone breaks into your house and tries to kidnap your daughter or kill your husband? What should you do? Should you shoot that person or act in a nonviolent way?" The answer depends on your state of being. If you are prepared, you may react calmly and intelligently, in the most nonviolent way possible. But to be ready to react with intelligence and nonviolence, you have to train yourself in advance. It may take ten years or longer. If you wait until the time of crisis to ask the question, it will be too late. A this-or-that kind of answer would be superficial. At that crucial moment, even if you know that nonviolence is better than violence, if your understanding is only intellectual and not in your whole being, you will not act nonviolently. The fear and anger in you will prevent you from acting in the most nonviolent way.

To prevent war, to prevent the next crisis, we must begin right now. When a war or a crisis has begun, it is already too late. If we and our children practice ahimsa in our daily lives, if we learn how to plant seeds of peace and reconciliation in our own hearts and minds, we will begin to establish real peace and, in that way, we may be able to prevent the next war. If another war does come, we will know that we have done our best. Is ten years enough time to prepare ourselves and our nation to avoid another war? How much time does it take to breathe consciously, to smile, and to be fully present in each moment? Our real enemy is forgetfulness. If we nourish mindfulness every day and water the seeds of peace in ourselves and those around us, we have a good chance to prevent the next war and to defuse the next crisis.

ELEVEN

If You Want Peace, Peace Is with You Immediately, 1988

Thich Nhat Hanh's experience of the 1976 Vietnamese refugee crisis is the basis for this essay, which was published in his book *The Sun My Heart*.

Twenty years ago, I wrote four Chinese characters on a paper lamp-shade: "If you want peace, peace is with you immediately." A few years later, in Singapore, I had the chance to practice these words.

It was 1976, and several of us were conducting an operation to rescue boat people in the Gulf of Siam.* The project was called "When blood is shed, we all suffer." At that time, not many people

---

* After the war ended in 1975, "boat people" began fleeing Vietnam by sea in order to avoid persecution at the hands of the new government. The refugees' first destinations were Hong Kong and the Southeast Asian locations of Indonesia, Malaysia, the Philippines, Singapore, and Thailand. Due to economic and political factors, Southeast Asian countries became increasingly unwilling to accept boat people on their shores. Over the course of twenty years, almost 800,000 refugees were successfully relocated in this way; approximately 400,000 others perished at sea.

knew about the presence of the boat people, and the governments of Thailand, Malaysia, and Singapore would not allow them to land on their shores. The practice was to push the boat people back out to sea so they would die, and those on land would not have to deal with them.

We hired two large ships—the *Leapdal* and the *Roland*—to pick up refugees on the open sea and two small ships—the *Saigon 200* and the *Blackmark*—to communicate between the larger ships and to transport water, food, medicine, and supplies. Our plan was to fill the two large ships with refugees and take them to Australia and Guam, where, on arrival, we would inform the press so that the world would take notice of their plight, and they would not be sent back. In Malaysia, Indonesia, and other countries, thousands of boat people had been sent back, and many of them died in the sea. We had to do our work in secret since the governments of the world did not want to acknowledge the plight of the boat people, and we knew we would be deported from Singapore if we were discovered.

We managed to rescue nearly eight hundred boat people from the Gulf of Siam. On New Year's Eve, I rode out to sea in the small *Saigon 200* to talk with the refugees on the larger ships. Using a wireless telephone, I wished them a happy New Year. After we said good-bye, I headed back to shore, and, in the darkness, a huge wave welled up and drenched me. I had the impression that the power of darkness was warning me, "It is the fate of these people to die. Why are you interfering?"

Sometimes we asked fishermen to pick these boat people up during the night, and then we took them by taxi to the French embassy in Singapore. In the morning, they were discovered by the French ambassador, who was very kind. He called the police, knowing that because of his awareness of the presence of these people, they would get "illegal refugee" status. Even though they were put in prison, it was far better than being sent back to sea. Then we worked to help these people get accepted to go to France. We were trying to do many things to improve the situation.

From time to time, we saw things you cannot believe. In Malaysia, we met with a group of sixty people in a barracks. They had just destroyed their own boat so that the Malaysian police would not send them back out to sea, but the police were trying to repair their boat in order to do just that. When we saw these people, the men were just staring into empty space, and the women and children could not stop crying. One of them told us that they came with two boats. The Malaysian police had given them some water and told them to go to Singapore, where they would be welcomed, but this was not true—the Singaporeans always towed boats back out into the ocean no matter how dangerous it was for the boat people.

When the two boats tried to sail away from Malaysia, one capsized. The sixty people on the other boat witnessed the deaths of everyone on the capsized boat, right in front of their eyes, and there was nothing they could do to help. So they decided to return to the shores of Malaysia, and this time they destroyed and sank their own boat the moment they arrived. They did not want to be pushed out to sea again. We immediately went to the nearest town and called Reuters, *Agence France-Presse*, and other media people to come and take photographs. Because of this, the police did not send them back out to sea, but instead brought them to prison and later to a refugee camp.

The suffering we touched doing this kind of work was so deep that if we did not have a reservoir of spiritual strength, we would not have been able to continue. During those days, we practiced sitting and walking meditation, and eating our meals in silence in a very concentrated way. We knew that without this kind of discipline, we would fail in our work. The lives of many people depended on our mindfulness.

After we had rescued nearly eight hundred people from small boats at sea, the government of Singapore discovered us. We were close to succeeding in sending the *Roland* and the *Leapdal* to Australia, but because of a leak to the press, several reporters tracked us down and published a story about our project. The press is sometimes frivolous; they just want to write a story, even if human lives are at stake.

Because we had been exposed, the Singapore authorities gave the order for the police to surround our flat at two o'clock in the morning. Two policemen were at the front door, two at the back, and two came in to get me. They took my travel documents and ordered me to leave the country within twenty-four hours. I knew that two large boatloads of people were waiting for me to help bring them to shore. The police said, "We will return your travel documents at the airport tomorrow." Those policemen were not like human beings. They were unable to understand the suffering of the boat people or how we were trying to help them.

What could we do in such a situation? We had to breathe deeply and consciously. Otherwise, we might panic, or fight with the police, or do something to express our anger at their lack of humanity. Knowing that in twenty-four hours we had to leave eight hundred people on two boats without food and water, what could we do? We could not go back to sleep.

At that time of the night, no one would answer phone calls. Even the French embassy was not open. So all of us practiced walking meditation inside our small flat for the rest of the night. If you practice conscious breathing before some difficulty arises, you will be prepared.

We had to find a way for eight hundred people to travel safely to Australia or Guam. The *Saigon 200* and the *Blackmark* were not allowed to leave port to take food and water to the refugees on the *Leapdal* and the *Roland*. The *Roland* had enough fuel to reach Australia, but we needed to get food to them. Then its engine broke down. The day was very windy and the sea quite rough, and we worried about their safety, even just drifting offshore. But the Malaysian government would not allow the ship to enter Malaysian waters. I tried to get permission to enter a neighboring country in order to continue the rescue operation, but the governments of Thailand, Malaysia, and Indonesia would not grant me an entry visa. Even though I was on land, I too was drifting on the sea, and my life was one with the eight hundred refugees on the ships. There were more problems than seemed possible to solve in just twenty-four hours.

I decided to practice the meditation topic "If you want peace, peace is with you immediately," and I was surprised to find myself quite calm, not afraid or worried about anything. I was not just being careless. This was truly a peaceful state of mind, and in that state, I was able to overcome this difficult situation. The idea came to me to ask the French embassy to intervene on my behalf so that my visa would be extended a few more days, enough time to tie up all of these loose ends. And at five minutes before noon, just as the Immigration Department was about to close for the weekend and I would have to leave the country, the extension was granted. As long as I live, I will never forget those seconds of sitting meditation, those breaths, those mindful steps during that night and that morning. Success came when I faced the problem directly. I vowed that if I could not have peace at that moment, I would never be able to have peace. If I could not be peaceful in the midst of danger, the kind of peace I might realize in easier times would not mean anything. With the practice "If you want peace, peace is with you immediately," I was able to resolve many problems one after another.

We had to hand the refugees over to the United Nations High Commissioner for Refugees, who kept them for months and years in the camps in Malaysia. It was very painful. Yet we had conducted our operation in meditation because we knew that everything depended on our mindfulness. We did sitting meditation late into the night every night, then recited the Heart Sutra, as if we were in a monastery.

Our work did bring the cries of the boat people to the attention of the world. In 1977, the US government increased the quota for Vietnamese refugees to seven thousand per year, then fifteen thousand, then one hundred thousand. Australia and other countries followed suit. If we do our best, in full awareness and with a heart free from anger, we cannot worry about results.

TWELVE

To Veterans, 1989

Thich Nhat Hanh's essay of encouragement and reconciliation for veterans was adapted from two public talks given during special retreats for veterans at Casa de Maria, Santa Barbara, California in May 1989 and Omega Institute, Rhinebeck, New York in June 1991.

In Massachusetts, Jon Kabat-Zinn read an insight poem that said, "The Vietnam War ends today." That was in 1987, and since then, I have begun to lead retreats for war veterans. I want veterans to realize how important they are.

I, too, am a veteran. I lost many friends—many brothers and sisters—during the Vietnam War, and I experienced much suffering. Grenades were thrown into my room but were deflected by a curtain. Social service workers under my direction were killed and maimed. We did our best to confront the violence with love, but we had to cry a lot. I have been practicing to transform my suffering and share my insight with others. I do not feel any more blame. I feel peace and compassion, and that allows me to help other people.

Veterans are the light at the tip of the candle, illuminating the way for the whole nation. If veterans can achieve awareness, transformation, understanding, and peace, they can share with the rest of society the realities of war. And they can teach us how to make peace with ourselves and each other so we never have to use violence to resolve conflicts again. To make the world a more peaceful place, to assure our children and grandchildren a life worth living, we need a transformation.

When you touch fire and your hand gets burned, it is not the responsibility of your hand alone. It is the responsibility of the whole person. The hand did not touch the fire by itself. It was commanded to do so by the brain, and the whole body got hurt at the same time. If the body blames the hand, that is not just. The hand acted because the body ordered it to do so. Why blame just the hand? When there is good communication between the hand and the rest of the body, both the hand and the body will feel better. If the body says, "You must bear the fruit; I cannot forgive you because of what you have done," that is a lack of understanding.

When you went to war, you went for the whole nation. The whole nation is responsible for what happens there, not you alone. Your hand was the hand of the whole nation. If you made mistakes, the whole nation made a mistake. If you went to war believing you were doing something important—trying to save a people, fighting evil—it was not your thinking alone; it was the thinking of the whole nation. You were sent there to fight, destroy, kill, and die. You are not the only one responsible. We cannot just shout at you and say, "You did that!" We all did it collectively.

Our individual consciousness is a product of our society, ancestors, education, and many other factors. Your sense of duty, service, and freedom were handed to you by society, and you went to war as representatives of your people, not just as individuals. You have to look deeply to understand what really happened. Your personal healing will be the healing of the whole nation, your children and their children.

When the hand gets burned, if there is good communication with the rest of the body, blood and other fluids will rush to the wound and begin the process of healing. If the nation comes to understand the true nature of the war, loving kindness will begin to surface, and healing will begin. As long as there is no communication, there is no insight or compassion, and you will continue to suffer. Non-veterans do not understand veterans, and they refuse to listen to you. You know the truth about war, but you have not been able to share your insight with them. You have suffered so much, but you have not been able to find ways to tell people about it, and they have not been ready to listen.

You continue to suffer because you feel guilty about your actions in Vietnam. Shame, guilt, and regret can be helpful or harmful; it depends how you use them. When you realize that you have caused a lot of damage, if you vow not to do it again, that regret is wholesome and beneficial. But if your guilt persists for too long and becomes a complex, it blocks the way to joy and peace. The way to liberate yourself is to look deeply into the nature of the guilt and self-hatred and see the seeds of the suffering—your ancestors, your parents, and the violence and lack of understanding in our society and its institutions. If you went to Vietnam with such a heritage of suffering, your actions were dictated by those forces. That is also true of those who opposed the war.

The seeds of our suffering come from many directions. When your parents conceived you, you already had many seeds of happiness and suffering handed down by your ancestors. In your mother's womb, you received more seeds. If your parents were not happy together, you received seeds of suffering.

As you grew up, if our parents argued and made each other unhappy, you received those seeds of suffering, too. If your parents were alcoholic, they made you suffer. If your father abused you, you suffered. Violent films and TV programs also watered the seeds of fear and hatred in you. By the time you became a soldier, you were already filled with suffering. Then, in the army you were told that the Vietnamese were beasts and you had to kill them. You cannot kill another human being without visualizing him as a beast. The mass media reinforced this image, watering the seeds of hatred and fear in order to help you kill. So many seeds of violence were watered before you were a soldier and during the time you were a soldier.

With such a heritage of suffering, it is no surprise that you committed atrocities during the war. You knew you could be killed at any time. You saw your friends killed in ambushes. You became more and more angry and more and more afraid. You may have killed children and women. You may have raped women or destroyed villages out of the fear, hatred, and rage that were pouring into you from so many directions. If you committed atrocities in Vietnam, it was the act of everyone—your father who abused you, the press, your commander, everyone who watered the seeds of anger in you so you could kill.

We do not need to go to overseas to a war zone to see such violence. The Los Angeles policeman beating Rodney King, that was also Vietnam. War manifests itself in so many ways here and now. It is a reflection of our collective consciousness, which is filled with suffering. With this heritage, the violence will repeat itself over and over. There will be other Vietnams, other Gulf Wars. It is our task to look deeply into the violence, hatred, and fear to see their roots.

Many soldiers who went to Vietnam had almost no contact with the Vietnamese people, culture, or life. They were told that the Vietnamese needed to be killed because they were evil killers. Because it was a high-tech war, you just pushed buttons to complete many of your missions. You did not know or see the damage you were inflicting on the people and the country of Vietnam. If you flew one hundred missions, you might have been successful as a soldier, but you did not know what was happening on the ground because you were so far away. Once you realized what was happening on the ground, you began to have guilt.

Who did the bombing? Your president, your congress, your senate, your people, everyone. You were only the hand ordered to do that. Why keep the regret for yourself? Why keep the shame for yourself? When you begin to see that, you will be free, and we need you to share your insight with everyone so we will not be tempted to do it again.

When you came home after the war, the American people were cool, neglectful, and unappreciative, and of course you became angry. But your people did not know anything about the war. Both the hawks and the doves had a very wrong view. You experienced the reality firsthand, and when you see that they were speaking out of ignorance, you will stop being angry at them. You were ignorant too, but now you have learned, and you are liberated from your anger. Now you can offer your compassion.

We who have experienced war directly have a responsibility to share our insight concerning the truth of war. We are the light at the tip of the candle. It is very hot, but it has the power of shining and illuminating. We can gather into groups to support each other. Practicing mindfulness, we will know how to look deeply into the nature of the war and, with our insight, awaken our own people. We know what war is. We also know that the war is not only in us; it is in everyone—veterans and non-veterans. We must share our insight, not out of anger, but out of love. Our people need us to do it. I am trying my best, and I hope my friends will do the same.

During the war, one portion of the American population had to confront one portion of the Vietnamese population. These were the soldiers, the combatants. But combatants and the non-combatants were not so different. In both, there were conflicts, and we have to look deeply to recognize these conflicts so that we can transform them into understanding and compassion, the fruit of insight. Insight can be brought about by mindfulness and looking deeply. If we do not have enough mindfulness, if we do not make enough effort to look deeply, we will not have enough insight to transform the conflicts that are within us, not to mention those between people and those with other nations.

The basic condition for happiness is to be understood. Our pain, hope, and despair have to be understood by someone for us to be happy. Vietnam veterans do not feel understood by their society, not even by members of their own families. Consciously or unconsciously, veterans blame non-veterans for not understanding them. There is so much misunderstanding to be dissolved. Veterans have suffered so much, and they have to take the time to understand their own suffering. It may look as if the people of America understand Gulf War veterans better, but I don't think so. Our ignorance about the nature of war is exactly the same. The war in Vietnam and the war in the Gulf were the same. The nature of war does not change just by the way people welcome you back. Whether they shout at you or wave flags and welcome you, the true nature of war is the same. We have to see that.

Many years have now passed since the Vietnam War. We are calm enough to realize that the Vietnam War was not necessary. We spent so much energy, so many human lives—millions of people died in Vietnam. There are still a lot of mines and bombs there that have not been defused, and there are also many bombs in our souls that have not been defused. We need to defuse the bombs in our souls first. Then we can go to Vietnam to help defuse the bombs there.

When we look deeply, we can see that all wars have their roots in a lack of understanding. We may be a little wiser now that twenty years have passed since the Vietnam War, but are we wise enough to prevent another war? In fact, we have already had another unnecessary war. To prevent yet another, we have to be prepared. We need time, of course, but we also need a way. If we know what to do, how to prepare, time is of secondary importance. We have to practice in a way that helps the whole nation see deeply into the nature of the war.

When you look into your consciousness and see your own pain, you also see the suffering and confusion of your society and your government. You have been embracing your suffering for many years, but when you see it directly, it will transform itself into a positive source of energy that will empower you to share your insight. To help others, we have to go to them with arms extended, filled with loving kindness and compassion. Blaming others or blaming ourselves can never help. The moment we have this insight, we will stop blaming, we will stop suffering, and we will have the energy to serve our people, even if they are still ignorant about the nature of war.

No one ever wins a war. The Vietnamese did not win the war. Millions of people in Vietnam are still suffering, and the country has been destroyed. Vietnam did not win anything. We cannot call it a victory. You cannot call the Gulf War a victory either. But many Americans did call it a victory so they could have the feeling once again that America is the greatest power on Earth. They organized parades welcoming the soldiers back, trying to overcome what they called a defeat many years ago.

I don't see any difference between a Vietnam veteran and a Gulf War veteran. I don't see any difference between the nature of the war in Vietnam and the nature of the Gulf War. I don't see any difference between the consciousness of the people during the Vietnam War and the consciousness of the people during the Gulf War. Please look deeply and remove all of these false distinctions. Look deeply to see the true nature of our society and our collective consciousness. If the people are educated, if the truth can break into their souls, we will all be able to go in the direction of peace.

As long as the American people believe that the Gulf War was moral, just, and liberating, they will be tempted to do the same thing the next time there is a conflict. How can we prevent that? By telling the truth, by sharing our insight. We need to look deeply and to share our insights. We do not have time to embrace our pain in private anymore. We have to reveal ourselves. We have to allow ourselves to be the light at the tip of the candle and to join with other veterans. We who have had firsthand experience can share the reality with everyone.

Transformation is the key. Looking just into the ocean of suffering, you see that it is immense. But if you turn around, you see the land. It is possible to transform our hearts right in the present moment. If we do, if we vow to go in the direction of peace and service, a rose will be born in us at that very moment. My brothers and sisters who died during the war have been reborn as flowers. We have to harvest those flowers and form a beautiful bouquet. Please don't dwell on your memory of guilt. If we can learn from our suffering, all those flowers will smile deeply at us, and we will be free.

I wrote this poem during the war. Like you, I suffered a lot, but transformation was taking place right there in the midst of the war. I know you can do the same.

MESSAGE

Life has left her footprints on my forehead.
But I have become a child again this morning.
The smile, seen through leaves and flowers,
is back to smooth away the wrinkles,
as the rain wipes away footprints on the beach.
Again, a cycle of birth and death begins.

I walk on thorns, but firmly, as among flowers.
I keep my head high.
Rhymes bloom among the sounds of bombs and mortars.
The tears I shed yesterday have become rain.
I feel calm hearing its sound on the thatched roof.
Childhood, my birth land, is calling me,
and the rain melts my despair.

I am still here alive, able to smile quietly.
O sweet fruit brought forth by the tree of suffering!
Carrying the dead body of my brother,
I go across the rice field in the darkness.
Earth will keep you tight within her arms, my dear,
so that tomorrow, you will be transformed into flowers,
those flowers smiling quietly in this morning field.
This moment you will weep no more, my dear.
We have gone through too deep a night.

This morning,
I kneel down on the grass,
when I notice your presence.
Flowers that carry the marvelous smile of ineffability
speak to me in silence.

The message,
the message of love
and understanding
has indeed come to us.

THIRTEEN

A Peaceful Heart, 1991

From a public talk Thich Nhat Hanh gave at Plum Village in March 1991.

Immediately after ordering a ground attack on Iraq, in February 1991, President Bush addressed his nation, saying, "Whatever you are doing at this moment, please stop and pray for our soldiers in the Gulf. God Bless the United States of America." I suspect that at the same moment many Moslems were also praying to their God to protect Iraq and the Iraqi soldiers. How could God know which nation to support? Many people pray to God because they want God to fulfill their needs. If they want to have a picnic, they may ask God for a clear, sunny day. At the same time, farmers who need more rain might pray for the opposite. If the weather is clear, the picnickers may say, "God is on our side; he answered our prayers." But if it rains, the farmers will say that God heard *their* prayers. This is the way we usually pray.

In the Sermon on the Mount, Jesus taught, "Blessed *are* the peacemakers: for they shall be called the children of God" (Matt. 5:9).[*]

---

[*] All biblical verses are from the Authorized (King James) Version.

Those who work for peace must have a peaceful heart. When you have a peaceful heart, you are the child of God. But many who work for peace are not at peace. They still have anger and frustration, and their work is not really peaceful. We cannot say that they belong to the Kingdom of God.

To preserve peace, our hearts must be at peace with the world, with our brothers and our sisters. When we try to overcome evil with evil, we are not working for peace. If you say, "Saddam Hussein is evil. We have to prevent him from continuing to be evil," and if you then use the same means he has been using, you are exactly like him. Trying to overcome evil with evil is not the way to make peace.

Jesus also said, "Thou shalt not kill; and whosoever shall kill shall be in danger of the judgment. But I say unto you, that whosoever is angry with his brother without a cause shall be in danger of the judgment ... whosoever shall say, Thou fool, shall be in danger of hell fire" (Matt. 5:21–22). Jesus did not say that if you are angry with your brother, you will be put in a place called hell. He said that if you are angry with your brother, you are already in hell. Anger *is* hell. He also said that you don't need to kill with your body to be put in jail. You need only to kill in your mind and you are already there.

In the Persian Gulf, many people practiced killing in their minds—Iraqi, American, French, British, and other soldiers. They knew that if they didn't kill, the enemy soldiers would kill them, so they used sandbags to represent their enemy, and holding their bayonets firmly, they ran, shouted, and plunged the bayonets into the sandbags. They practiced killing day and night in their hearts and minds. The damage caused by that kind of practice is huge. I happened to see a few seconds of that kind of practice on TV. Even if President Bush had not given the order for a land offensive, a lot of damage was already being done in the minds and hearts of one million people in the Gulf. Those kinds of wounds last for a long time and are transmitted to future generations. If you train yourself every day to kill during the day and then dream of killing during the night because you have spent so much time concentrating on that, the damage is deep. If you survive, you will bear that kind of scar for many years. This is a real tragedy. We usually count bodies to measure the damage from a war, but we don't count these kinds of wounds in the hearts and minds of so many soldiers. We have to see the real long-term damage that war causes. Soldiers live in hell day and night, even before they go into the battlefield and even after they return home.

We may think of peace as the absence of war, that if the great powers would reduce their weapons arsenals, we could have peace. But if we look deeply into the weapons, we will see our own minds— our own prejudices, fears, and ignorance. Even if we transport all the bombs to the moon, the roots of war and the roots of the bombs are still here—in our hearts and minds—and, sooner or later, we will make new bombs. To work for peace is to uproot war from ourselves and from the hearts of men and women. To start a war and give the opportunity to one million men and women to practice killing day and night in their hearts is to plant many, many seeds of war—anger, frustration, and the fear of being killed. I felt very sad when I learned that more than 80 percent of the American people supported the Gulf War.

—

Ye have heard that it hath been said, Thou shalt love thy neighbor, and hate thine enemy. But I say unto you, Love your enemies, bless

them that curse you, do good to them that hate you, and pray for
them which despitefully use you, and persecute you; that ye may be
the children of your Father who is in heaven: for he maketh his sun to
rise on the evil and on the good, and sendeth rain on the just and on
the unjust. (Matt. 5:39–40)

This is Jesus's teaching about revenge. When someone asks you for something, give it to him. When he wants to borrow something from you, lend it to him. How many Christians actually practice this? There is a story about an American soldier who was taking a Japanese prisoner during World War II. While walking together, the American discovered that the Japanese soldier spoke English and that he had been a Christian before he abandoned his faith. So he asked, "Why did you abandon Christianity? It is an excellent religion," and the Japanese man said, "I could not become a soldier and continue to be a Christian. I don't think a good Christian can become a soldier and kill another person." He understood this passage from Matthew. There must be ways to solve our conflicts without having to resort to killing. We must focus our attention on this. We have to find ways to help people get out of difficult situations, situations of conflict, without having to kill.

—

Ye have heard that it hath been said, Thou shalt love thy neighbor,
and hate thine enemy. But I say unto you, Love your enemies, bless
them that curse you, do good to them that hate you, and pray for
them which despitefully use you, and persecute you; That ye may be
the children of your Father which is in heaven: for he maketh his sun
to rise on the evil and on the good, and sendeth rain on the just and
on the unjust. (Matt. 5:43–45)

This is nondiscrimination. When you pray only for your own picnic and not for the farmers who need the rain, you are doing the opposite of what Jesus taught. Jesus said, "Love your enemies, bless them that curse you." When we look deeply into our anger, we see that the person we call our enemy is also suffering. As soon as we see that, we have the capacity of accepting and having compassion for them. Jesus called this "loving your enemy." When we are able to love our enemy, they're no longer our enemy. The idea of "enemy" vanishes and is replaced by the notion of someone suffering a great deal who needs our compassion. Doing this is sometimes easier than we might think, but we need to practice. If we read the Bible but don't practice, it will not help much.

—

Forgive us our trespasses, as we forgive those who trespass against us. (Matt. 6:12)

Everyone makes mistakes. If we are mindful, we see that some of our actions in the past may have caused others to suffer, and some actions of others have made us suffer. We want to be forgiving. We want to begin anew. "You, my brother or sister, have wronged me in the past. I now understand that it was because you were suffering and did not see clearly. I no longer feel anger towards you." That kind of forgiveness is the fruit of awareness. When you are mindful you can see all the causes that led the other person to make you suffer. When you see this, forgiveness and release arise naturally. You can't force yourself to forgive. Only when you understand what has happened can you have compassion for the other person and forgive them.

If President Bush had had more understanding of the mind of President Hussein, peace might have been obtained. President

Gorbachev made a number of proposals that could have been acceptable to the allies, and many lives could have been spared. But because anger was there, Mr. Bush rejected Mr. Gorbachev's proposals, and Mr. Hussein gave the order to burn Kuwaiti oil wells. If President Bush had seen clearly the suffering of the Iraqi people, he would not have allowed his anger to be expressed by starting a war. He asked the American people to pray for the allied soldiers. He asked God to bless the United States of America. He did not say that we should pray for the civilians in Iraq or even the people of Kuwait. He wanted God to be on the side of America.

80 percent of the American people called the Persian Gulf War a victory—only a few hundred American soldiers were killed. But every human life is precious, and the loss of the one hundred thousand or more Iraqi people was a great tragedy! You may identify yourself as an American, but that is only partially true. You are more than that. You may have lost just a few hundred American lives, but you also suffered from the Gulf War in many other ways. The death of so many Iraqi soldiers and civilians are also casualties that America suffered, because their death was your country's work. When President Bush said, "God bless the United States of America," he was not paying enough attention to the lives of non-Americans. To those of us who are not American, this was not a good image of America. It was selfish and arrogant, and this was also a casualty that America suffered—not just by guns and bombs but by your President's statement. If the President had said, "God bless us so that the war will end soon and that Americans as well as Iraqis will suffer as little as possible," he could have won a lot more sympathy from people around the world. But he did not say that.

Who is President Bush? President Bush is us. We are responsible for the way he feels, for everything he does. 80 percent of the people in America supported him in this war. Why blame him? Our capacity of loving and understanding was so limited. We were not peaceful enough in our own hearts, and we were not able to bring peace to the hearts of other people. When I saw how we prepared for war and practiced killing day and night in our hearts and minds, I felt overwhelmed.

After the parades ended and the yellow ribbons were no longer there, what do we have? What did the wives, husbands, children, brothers, and sisters of the soldiers receive when their loved ones returned from the Gulf after so much fear, hatred, and killing, in reality and in their daily practice? We cannot imagine the long-term effects of watering so many seeds of war.

Please sit still, breathe, and look deeply, and you will see the real losses, the real casualties that America suffered and continues to suffer from the Persian Gulf War. Visualize the five hundred thousand allied soldiers stationed in Saudi Arabia, waiting for the order to invade Iraq, jumping and screaming as they plunged their bayonets into sandbags that represented Iraqi soldiers. You cannot plunge a bayonet into a person without first transforming yourself into a beast. On the other side, one million Iraqi soldiers were practicing the same. One and a half million soldiers were practicing violence, hatred, and fear, and the American public supported their doing so. They thought that this war was somehow clean, quick, and moral. They saw only bridges and buildings being destroyed, but the real casualties were the souls of the men and women who came home after practicing violence for so many months.

How could they do that and remain themselves? When they returned, the soldiers cried for joy: they were alive! Their parents, wives, husbands, children, and friends also cried for joy. But after one or two weeks, the war welled up from within their deepest consciousness, and their families and the whole of society will have to endure their pain for a long time. If you are a psychologist, a playwright, a novelist, a composer, a filmmaker, a lawyer, a legislator, a peacemaker, or an environmentalist, please look deeply into the souls of the soldiers who returned from the war so you can see the real suffering that war causes, not only to soldiers but to everyone. Then project that image onto a huge screen for the whole nation to see and to learn. If you are able to share the truth concerning the Gulf War, we will be able to avoid starting another war like it in the future. We have to see how deep the wounds of war are. How could anyone call the Gulf War a victory? A victory for whom?

FOURTEEN

The Roots of War, 1991

"The Roots of War" brings together Thich Nhat Hanh's public talks given in North America in the spring of 1991 during the first Gulf War (1990–1991).

There is a deep malaise in our society. Look at the way young people consume drugs. They use drugs as a way to forget. These are the seeds of war that we have to acknowledge if we want to transform them. We have to do it together, looking deeply into the nature of the war in our collective consciousness. The war is in our souls.

Many of us are not healthy within, and we continue to look for things that only harm us more. We come home from work exhausted, and we do not know how to relax. We feel a kind of vacuum in ourselves, so we turn on the television. We live in a society where we always feel we are lacking something, and we want to fill it. If we don't turn on the TV, we eat or read or talk on the telephone. We are always trying to fill our void with something. Some people do social or political work this way, but doing this only makes us less satisfied, hungrier, and we want to consume more. We feel alienated from ourselves. There is so much fear, hatred, and anger in us, and we want to suppress it, so we consume more and more things that only increase the level of toxicity already in us. We watch films filled with screaming and violence. We read magazines and novels filled with hatred and confusion. We do not even have the courage to turn off our TV, because we are afraid to go back to ourselves.

The night I heard President George H.W. Bush give the order to attack Iraq, I could not sleep. I was angry and overwhelmed. The next morning in the middle of my talk, I suddenly paused and announced, "I don't think I will go to North America this spring." The words just sprang out. Then I continued the talk. In the afternoon, one American student told me, "Thây, I think you have to go to the United States. Many friends there feel the same as you do, and it would help if you would go and support them." I did not say anything. I practiced breathing, walking, and sitting, and a few days later, I decided to go. I saw that I was one with the American people, George Bush, and Saddam Hussein. I had been angry with President Bush, but after breathing consciously and looking deeply, I saw myself as President Bush. I had not been practicing well enough to change this situation. I saw that Saddam Hussein was not the only person who had lit the oil wells in Kuwait. All of us reached out our hands and lit the oil wells with him.

In our collective consciousness, we have seeds of nonviolence, and President Bush did begin with sanctions. But we did not support and encourage him enough, so he switched to a more violent way. We cannot blame only him. The president acted the way he did because we acted the way we did. It is because we are not happy enough that we had a war. If we were happier, we would not take refuge in alcohol, drugs, war, and violence. Young people tell me that the most precious gift their parents can give is their own happiness.

If the parents themselves are happy, the children will receive seeds of happiness in their consciousness, and when they grow up, they will know how to make others happy too. When parents fight, they sow seeds of suffering in the hearts of their children, and with that kind of heritage, children grow up unhappy. These are the roots of war. If children are unhappy, they will look for other things that are exactly like war—alcohol, drugs, TV programs, magazines, films, and other violent "cultural products."

Our society is sick. When we put young people in this society without trying to protect them, they will receive violence, hatred, and fear every day and eventually get sick. Our conversations, our TV programs, our advertisements, our newspapers, our magazines all water the seeds of suffering in young people and not-so-young people.

How can we transform our individual consciousness and the collective consciousness of our society? How can we refrain from consuming more toxic cultural products? We need guidelines—a diet—and we need to practice watering the seeds of peace, joy, and happiness in us. The most important practice for preventing war is to stay in touch with what is refreshing, healing, and joyful inside us and all around us. If we practice walking mindfully—being in touch with the earth, the air, the trees, and ourselves—we can heal ourselves, and our entire society can also be healed. If the whole nation would practice watering seeds of joy and peace and not just seeds of anger and violence, the elements of war in all of us will be transformed.

We must prepare ourselves, whether we have one minute, ten years, or one thousand years. If we don't have time, there is no use discussing peace because you cannot practice peace without time. If you have one minute, please use that minute to breathe in and out calmly and plant the seeds of peace and understanding in yourself. If you have ten years, please use the ten years to prevent the next war. If you have one thousand years, please use the time to prevent the destruction of our planet.

Transformation is possible, but we need time. There are already seeds of peace in those we call "hawks," but they need us to help water these seeds of peace and understanding, or else their seeds of anger and aggression will continue to dominate them. Do not feel discouraged. Just by your way of looking at things and doing things, you influence others. Approach everyone with love and patience, and try to water the positive seeds in them. We have to help each other, being skillful, kind, and understanding. Blaming and arguing never helps.

People all over the world saw the Los Angeles policemen beating Rodney King. When I first saw that video on French TV, I felt that I was the one who was beaten, and I suffered a lot. I think you must have felt the same. We were all victims of the violence, anger, misunderstanding, and the lack of respect for our human dignity.

But as I looked more deeply, I saw that the policemen beating Rodney King were no different from myself. They were acting so violently because our society is filled with hatred and violence. Everything is like a time bomb ready to explode, and we are all part of that bomb; we are all co-responsible. We are all the policemen *and* the victim.

In the practice of mindfulness, we nurture the ability to look deeply into the nature of things and people, and the fruit we gain is insight, understanding, and love. Because we have not practiced deeply enough, violence has become the substance of our society. Putting the policemen in jail will not solve this fundamental problem. We accept violence as a way of life and a way to deal with problems. If we are not mindful—if we do not transform our shared suffering through compassion and deep understanding—then one day our child will be the one who is beaten, or the one doing the beating. It is very much our affair. We have to go deeper than the surface to see the roots of the problem.

FIFTEEN

The Sun My Heart, 1992

Parts of Thich Nhat Hanh's meditative essay on the interconnected-ness of all life, *The Sun My Heart*, appeared in the Plum Village community journal *The Mindfulness Bell* in 1992.

When I first left Vietnam, I had a dream in which I was a young boy, smiling and at ease in my own land, surrounded by my own people in a time of peace. There was a beautiful hillside, lush with trees and flowers, and on it was a little house. But each time I approached the hillside, obstacles prevented me from climbing it, and then I woke up.

The dream recurred many times. I continued to do my work and to practice mindfulness, trying to be in touch with the beautiful trees, people, flowers, and sunshine that surrounded me in Europe and North America. I looked deeply at these things, and I played under the trees with the children exactly as I had in Vietnam. After a year, the dream stopped. Seeds of acceptance and joy had been planted in me, and I began to look at Europe, America, and other countries in Asia as also my home. I realized that my home is the Earth. Whenever I felt homesick for Vietnam, I went outside into a backyard or a park, and found a place to practice breathing, walking, and smiling among the trees.

But some cities had very few trees, even then. I can imagine someday soon a city with no trees at all. Imagine a city that has only one tree left. People there become mentally ill because they are so alienated from nature. Then one doctor in the city sees why people are getting sick, and he offers each person who comes to him this prescription: "You are sick because you are cut off from Mother Nature. Every morning, take a bus, go to the tree in the center of the city, and hug it for fifteen minutes. Look at the beautiful tree with green leaves and smell its fragrant bark."

After three months of practicing this, the patient will feel much better. But because many people suffer from the same malady and the doctor always gives the same prescription, after a short time, the line of people waiting their turn to embrace the tree gets to be very long, more than a mile, and people begin to get impatient. Fifteen minutes is now too long for each person to hug the tree, so the city council legislates a five-minute maximum. Then they have to shorten it to one minute, and then only a few seconds. Finally, there is no remedy at all for the sickness.

If we are not mindful, we may find ourselves in that situation soon. We have to remember that our body is not limited to what lies inside the boundary of our skin. Our body is limitless. We know that if our heart stops beating, the flow of our life will stop, but we do not often take the time to notice the many things outside of our bodies that are equally essential for our survival. If the ozone layer around our Earth were to disappear even for an instant, we would die. If the sun were to stop shining, the flow of our life would stop. The sun is our second heart, our heart outside of our body. It gives all life on Earth the warmth necessary for existence. Plants live thanks to the sun. Their leaves absorb the sun's energy, along with carbon dioxide from the air, to produce food for the tree or the flower. And thanks to plants, we and other animals can live. All of us—people, animals, plants, and minerals—"consume" the sun, directly and indirectly. We cannot begin to describe all the effects of the sun, that great heart outside of our body.

When we look at green vegetables, we should know that it is the sun that is green and not just the vegetables. The green color in the leaves of the vegetables is due to the presence of the sun. Without the sun, no species of living being could survive. Without sun, water, air, and soil, there would be no vegetables. The vegetables are the coming together of many conditions near and far.

There is no phenomenon in the universe that does not intimately concern us, from a pebble resting at the bottom of the ocean to the movement of a galaxy millions of light years away. Walt Whitman said, "I believe a blade of grass is no less than the journey-work of the stars." These words are not philosophy. They come from the depths of his soul. He also said, "I am large, I contain multitudes."

This might be called the meditation on "interbeing endlessly interwoven." All phenomena are interdependent. When we think of a speck of dust, a flower, or a human being, our habitual thinking cannot break loose from the idea of calculation. We see a line drawn between one and many, one and not one. But if we truly realize the interdependent nature of the dust, the flower, and the human being, we see that unity cannot exist without diversity. Unity and diversity interpenetrate each other freely. Unity is diversity, and diversity is unity. This is the principle of interbeing.

If you are a mountain climber or someone who enjoys the countryside or the forest, you know that forests are our lungs outside of our bodies. Yet we have been living in a way that has allowed millions of square miles of land to be deforested, and we have also destroyed the air, the rivers, and parts of the ozone layer. We are imprisoned in our small selves, thinking only of creating comfortable conditions for this small self, while destroying our larger self. If we want to change the situation, we must begin by being our true selves. To be our true selves means we have to *be* the forest, the river, and the ozone layer. If we visualize ourselves as the forest, we will experience the hopes and fears of the trees. If we don't do this, the forests will die, and we will lose our chance for peace. When we understand that we inter-are with the trees, we will know that it is up to us to make an effort to keep the trees alive. In the last twenty years, our automobiles and factories have created acid rain that has destroyed so many trees. Because we inter-are with the trees, we know that if they cannot live, we too will disappear very soon.

We humans think we are smart, but an orchid, for example, knows how to produce noble, symmetrical flowers, and a snail knows how to make a beautiful, well-proportioned shell. Compared with their knowledge, ours is not worth much at all. We should bow deeply before the orchid and the snail and join our palms reverently before the monarch butterfly and the magnolia tree. The feeling of respect for all species will help us recognize the noblest nature in ourselves.

An oak tree is an oak tree. That is all an oak tree needs to do. If an oak tree is less than an oak tree, we will all be in trouble. In our former lives, we were rocks, clouds, and trees. We have also been an oak tree. This is not just Buddhist thought; it is scientific. We humans are a young species. At one time we were plants, we were trees, and now we have become humans. We have to remember our past existences and be humble. We can learn a lot from an oak tree.

All life is impermanent. We are all children of the Earth, and, at some time, she will take us back to her again. We are continually arising from Mother Earth, being nurtured by her, and then returning to the Earth. Like us, plants are born, live for a while, and then return to the Earth. When they decompose, they fertilize our gardens. Living vegetables and decomposing vegetables are part of the same reality. Without one, the other cannot be. After six months, compost becomes fresh vegetables again. Plants and the Earth rely on each other. Whether the Earth is fresh, beautiful, and green or arid and parched depends on the plants.

It also depends on us. Our way of walking on the Earth has a great influence on animals and plants. We have killed so many animals and plants and destroyed their environment. Many are now extinct. In turn, our environment is now harming all of us. We are like sleepwalkers, not knowing what we are doing or where we are heading. Whether we can wake up or not depends on whether we can walk mindfully on our Mother Earth. The future of all life, including our own, depends on our mindful steps.

Birds' songs express joy, beauty, and purity, and evoke in us vitality and love. So many beings in the universe love us unconditionally. The trees, the water, and the air don't ask anything of us; they just love us. Even though we need this kind of love, we continue to destroy them. By destroying the animals, the air, and the trees, we are destroying ourselves. We must learn to practice unconditional love for all beings so that the animals, the air, the trees, and the minerals can continue to be themselves.

Our ecology should be a deep ecology—not only deep, but universal. There is pollution in our consciousness. Television, films, and newspapers are forms of pollution for us and our children. They sow seeds of violence and anxiety in us and pollute our consciousness, just as we destroy our environment by farming with chemicals, clear-cutting the trees, and polluting the water. We need to protect the ecology of the Earth and the ecology of the mind, or this kind of violence and recklessness will spill over into even more areas of life.

Our Earth, our green beautiful Earth, is in danger, and all of us know it. Yet we act as if our daily lives have nothing to do with the situation of the world. If the Earth were your body, you would be able to feel many areas where she is suffering. Many people are aware of the world's suffering, and their hearts are filled with compassion. They know what needs to be done, and they engage in political, social, and environmental work to try to change things. But after a period of intense involvement, they become discouraged because they lack the strength needed to sustain a life of action. Real strength is not in power, money, or weapons but in deep, inner peace. If we change our daily lives—the way we think, speak, and act—we change the world. The best way to take care of the environment is to take care of the environmentalist.

Many Buddhist teachings help us understand our interconnectedness with our Mother, the Earth. One of the deepest is the Diamond Sutra, which is written in the form of a dialogue between the Buddha and his senior disciple, Subhuti. It begins with this question by Subhuti: "If daughters and sons of good families wish to give rise to the highest, most fulfilled, awakened mind, what should they rely on and what should they do to master their thinking?" This is the same as asking, "If I want to use my whole being to protect life, what methods and principles should I use?"

The Buddha answers, "We have to do our best to help every living being cross the ocean of suffering. But after all beings have arrived at the shore of liberation, no being at all has been carried to the other shore. If you are still caught up in the idea of a self, a person, a living being, or a life span, you are not an authentic bodhisattva." Self, person, living being, and life span are four notions that prevent us from seeing reality.

Life is one. We do not need to slice it into pieces and call this or that piece a "self." What we call a self is made only of nonself elements. When we look at a flower, for example, we may think that it is different from "non-flower" things. But when we look more deeply, we see that everything else in the cosmos is in that flower. Without all of the non-flower elements—sunshine, clouds, earth, minerals, heat, rivers, and consciousness—a flower cannot be. That is why the Buddha teaches that the self does not exist. We have to discard all distinctions between self and nonself. How can anyone work to protect the environment without this insight?

The second notion that prevents us from seeing reality as it is the notion of a person, a human being. We usually discriminate between humans and non-humans, thinking that we are more important than other species. But since we humans are made of non-human elements, to protect ourselves we have to protect all of the non-human elements. There is no other way. If you think that God created man in his own image, and he created other things for man to use, you are already making the discrimination that man is more important than other things. When we see that humans have no self, we see that to take care of the environment (the non-human elements) is to take care of humanity. The best way to take good care of men and women so that they can be truly healthy and happy is to take care of the environment.

I know ecologists who are not happy with their partners. They work hard to improve the environment, partly to escape their family life. If people are not happy within themselves, how can they help the environment? That is why the Buddha teaches that to protect the non-human elements is to protect humans, and to protect humans is to protect non-human elements.

The third notion we have to break through is the notion of a living being. We think that we living beings are different from inanimate objects, but according to the principle of interbeing, living beings are comprised of non-living-being elements. When we look into ourselves, we see minerals and all other non-living-being elements. Why discriminate against what we call inanimate? To protect living beings, we must protect the stones, the soil, and the oceans. Before the atomic bomb was dropped on Hiroshima, there were many beautiful stone benches in the parks. As the Japanese were rebuilding their city, they discovered that these stones were dead, so they carried them away and buried them. Then they brought in live stones. Do not think these things are not alive. Atoms are always moving. Electrons move at nearly the speed of light. According to the teaching of Buddhism, these atoms and stones are consciousness itself. That is why discrimination by living beings against non-living beings should be discarded.

The last notion is that of a life span. We think that we have been alive since a certain point in time and that prior to that moment, our life did not exist. This distinction between life and non-life is not correct. Life is made of death, and death is made of life. We have to accept death; it makes life possible. The cells in our body are dying every day, but we never think to organize funerals for them. The death of one cell allows for the birth of another. Life and death are two aspects of the same reality. We must learn to die peacefully so that others may live. This deep meditation brings forth non-fear, non-anger, and non-despair, the strengths we need for our work.

With non-fear, even when we see that a problem is huge, we will not burn out. We will know how to make small, steady steps. If those who work to protect the environment contemplate these four notions, they will know how to be and how to act.

In another beautiful Buddhist text, the Avatamsaka (Adorning the Buddha with Flowers) Sutra, the Buddha continues to elaborate his insights concerning our "interpenetration" with our environment. Please meditate with me on the "Ten Penetrations."

The first is "All worlds penetrate a single pore. A single pore penetrates all worlds." Look deeply at a flower. It may be tiny, but the sun, the clouds, and everything else in the cosmos penetrate it. Nuclear physicists say very much the same thing: one electron is made by all electrons; one electron is in all electrons.

The second penetration is "All living beings penetrate one body. One body penetrates all living beings." When you kill a living being, you kill yourself and everyone else as well.

The third is "Infinite time penetrates one second. One second penetrates infinite time." A *ksana* is the shortest period of time, actually much shorter than a second.

The fourth penetration is "All Buddhist teachings penetrate one teaching. One teaching penetrates all Buddhist teachings." As a young monk, I had the opportunity to learn that Buddhism is made of non-Buddhist elements. So, whenever I study Christianity or Judaism, I find the Buddhist elements in them, and vice versa. I always respect non-Buddhist teachings. All Buddhist teachings penetrate one teaching, and one teaching penetrates all Buddhist teachings. We are free.

The fifth penetration is "Innumerable spheres enter one sphere. One sphere enters innumerable spheres." A sphere is a geographical space. Innumerable spheres penetrate into one particular area, and one particular area enters into innumerable spheres. It means that when you destroy one area, you destroy every area. When you save one area, you save all areas. A student once asked me, "Thây, there are so many urgent problems, what should I do?" I said, "Take one thing and do it very deeply and carefully, and you will be doing everything at the same time."

The sixth penetration is "All sense organs penetrate one organ. One organ penetrates all sense organs"—eye, ear, nose, tongue, body, and mind. To take care of one means to take care of many. To take care of your eyes means to take care of the eyes of innumerable living beings.

The seventh penetration is "All sense organs penetrate non-sense organs. Non-sense organs penetrate all sense organs." Not only do non-sense organs penetrate sense organs, but they also penetrate non-sense organs. There is no discrimination. Sense organs are made of non-sense-organ elements. That is why they penetrate non-sense organs. This helps us remember the teaching of the Diamond Sutra.

The eighth penetration is "One perception penetrates all perceptions. All perceptions penetrate one perception." If your perception is not accurate, it will influence all other perceptions in yourself and others. Suppose a bus driver has an incorrect perception. We know what may happen. One perception penetrates all perceptions.

The ninth penetration is "Every sound penetrates one sound. One sound penetrates every sound." This is a very deep teaching. If we understand one sound or one word, we can understand all.

The tenth penetration is "All times penetrate one time. One time penetrates all times—past, present, and future. In one second, you can find the past, present, and future." In the past, you can see the present and the future. In the present, you can find the past and future. In the future, you can find the past and present. They "inter-contain" each other. Space contains time, time contains space. In the teaching of interpenetration, the one determines the other, the other determines the one. When we realize our nature of interbeing, we will stop blaming and killing because we know that we inter-are.

Interpenetration is an important teaching, but it still suggests that things that are outside of one another penetrate into each other. Interbeing is a step forward. We are already inside, so we don't have to enter. In contemporary nuclear physics, people talk about implicit order and explicit order. In the explicit order, things exist outside of each other—the table outside of the flower, the sunshine outside of the cypress tree. In the implicit order, we see that they are inside each other—the sunshine inside the cypress tree. Interbeing is the implicit order. To practice mindfulness and to look deeply into the nature of things is to discover the true nature of interbeing. We find peace, and we develop the strength to be in touch with everything. With this understanding, we can easily sustain the work of loving and caring for the Earth and for each other for a long time.

SIXTEEN

The Way Ahead for Buddhism in Vietnam, 1993

Thich Nhat Hanh drafted this call to action in 1992 to encourage religious freedom in Vietnam and sent it to high-ranking monks and nuns in the Buddhist leadership and to government authorities in Vietnam. It was printed in *The Mindfulness Bell*, Spring 1993.

1. *Protecting Our Nation's Natural Heritage*
   (Preserving Our Mother's Body)

As Vietnamese students of the Buddha, we make a vow to protect the integrity of the territory of Vietnam, which means to protect the soil, the mountains, the forests, the rivers, the ocean, and the air. We vow to do everything that we can to protect the environment, to protect every species of animal and plant life in the country of Vietnam. We vow to stop the pollution and destruction of the nature-heritage of Vietnam. As Vietnamese Buddhists we call on our compatriots, our government, and all those who are friends of Vietnam anywhere in the world to make a contribution to this task of protecting the Vietnamese environment. We expect that efforts to develop agriculture, industry, investments, and the exploitation of resources will be founded on the principle of protecting our nature-heritage.

The protection of life is a practice observed by all Buddhists. Life here means not only the life of human beings, but also the life of all animal, plant, and mineral species. The Diamond Sutra teaches that the human race cannot exist if there is destruction of the animal, plant, and mineral species. Anyone living anywhere on this planet, if they are aware of the state of our planet Earth at this present time, will look at the world and act in accord with this principle.

2. Protecting the Cultural Heritage of Our People
(Just as the Bird Has Its Nest, so We Have Ancestors)

As Vietnamese students of the Buddha, we vow to bear in mind the happiness established for us by our ancestors. We are determined not to abandon the cultural roots and traditions of our ancestors and our people. All of our cultural heritage—whether architecture (our pagodas, village meeting houses, villages, tombs, non-Buddhist temples and shrines), literature, poetry, music, dance, customs, or dress—needs to be respected, preserved, and cared for so that all our people, now and in the future, may be in touch with our traditional culture. We call on our compatriots, our government, and all those who are friends of Vietnam anywhere in the world to contribute their energy to this work of protecting our culture. New ways of thought, new ways of life, and new forms of religious belief should be introduced in the spirit of respecting and protecting our cultural heritage.

People of our age suffer and feel alienated because they have cut off all contact with their cultural roots. As Vietnamese Buddhists we call for a return to the source in order to rediscover a feeling of confidence in the value of our traditional culture, to foster that value, and to enrich it. An individual is not a separate, independent entity, but a continuation of the ancestral line, tradition, and culture. This fact is a reflection of the awareness of the teachings of interdependent origination and selflessness in Buddhism.

Anyone whosoever living anywhere on this planet Earth, if they are aware of the state of separation and alienation of people of our time, will look at the world and act in accord with this principle.

3. *Vietnamese Buddhists Have No Enemies*
   (Only Love and Compassion Can Put an End to Hatred)

Vietnamese students of the Buddha wish to live in peace in their own hearts and at peace with all other groups of the Vietnamese people, without discriminating according to race, creed, and ideology, sharing the willingness to protect the natural and cultural heritage of our land. As Vietnamese Buddhists, we look on every Vietnamese person as our brother or sister and do not consider anyone to be an enemy, even those who have contributed to the suppression of Buddhists in the past. We make the vow to contribute to the overcoming of all rivalries and resolving all misunderstandings between different sectors of our people. We appeal for understanding and forgiveness of mistakes which we have caused each other in the past in order to contribute together to building the present and the future. As Buddhists, it is our earnest desire to have peace and joy in our hearts by living in harmony with the Confucian, Taoist, Christian, Cao Dai, Hoa Hao, and any other religious traditions of our people.

Recognizing that no one is our enemy is one of the basic teachings of Buddhism. This recognition is also enshrined in all the great spiritual, humanist, and religious traditions of the world.

4. Buddhism as Engaged and Unified

As Vietnamese students of the Buddha, we wish to have a unified congregation which unites all the Buddhists of Vietnam. The Unified Buddhist Church of Vietnam (founded in 1964) and the Buddhist Church of Vietnam (founded in 1981) need to unite, to combine all the good and beautiful elements of these two churches.* A unified church of all Vietnamese Buddhists must be independent, autonomous, and not subject to government interference in its internal affairs.

The Unified Buddhist Church of Vietnam was one of the outstanding achievements of Vietnamese Buddhists after countless struggles which cost many tears and many lives. Such a church is truly a church of the people. Such a church has to be recognized by history, by the people, and by the government. The

---

* The Unified Buddhist Church (UBC) was founded in 1964 to unify the different sects of Vietnamese Buddhism which were present in the country at the time. The unification also came in response to government hostility towards Buddhists during the Vietnam War. In 1981, the new communist government consolidated all Buddhist organizations under the umbrella group the Buddhist Church of Vietnam (BCV). The UBC was banned within Vietnam, and it continues to operate in exile. To this day, BCV is the only Buddhist sangha recognized by the Vietnamese government.

strengths of such a church must be welcomed wholeheartedly by a unified Buddhist congregation of all Buddhists in Vietnam.

5. *Vietnamese Buddhism Has No Political Objective*

The Unified Buddhist Church of all Vietnamese Buddhists is determined to remain in the field of religious practice. The sole intent of all the teaching and practice activities of Vietnamese Buddhists is to heal the deep wounds of individuals, families, and society, and to transform suffering, hatred, and anger so that people will be able to accept, love, and embrace each other. We reject the path of seeking power, the manipulation of political power, or engagement in partisan politics.

6. *The Real Needs of Present-Day Buddhism in Vietnam*

As Vietnamese students of the Buddha, we expect the right to practice and teach in freedom just as religion is practiced in the free countries of the world. This includes

1. the freedom to publish and circulate Buddhist sutras, books, and journals;

2. the freedom to found institutes of all levels of Buddhist studies;

3. the freedom to found centers of study and practice for both laypeople and monks and nuns;

4. the freedom to organize ceremonies, teachings, and sessions of practice; and

5. the freedom to practice relief work in society as a way of realizing love and compassion.

In addition, Vietnamese Buddhists demand

6. that all imprisoned monks be set free;

7. that all establishments belonging to the Unified Buddhist Church that have been confiscated be returned;

8. that monks and nuns have the right to go abroad in order to study, make contacts, practice, and teach;

9. that all monks, nuns, and practitioners abroad have the right to come home to Vietnam to practice and to teach; and

10. that all the important figures of the Council of Elders and the Executive Council of the Unified Buddhist Church be allowed to return to their former positions of responsibility in the Unified Buddhist Church of all Vietnamese Buddhists.*

---

* For instance, Thich Huyen Quang (1919–2008) and Thich Quang Do (1928–2020), the Patriarchs of the Unified Buddhist Church, were jailed in the mid-1970s by the communist government. At that time, UBC facilities were seized, and documents were burned. After the formal establishment of the government-sanctioned Buddhist Church of Vietnam, Thich Huyen Quang and Thich Quang Do were placed on permanent house arrest and exiled, respectively.

SEVENTEEN

The Bells of Mindfulness, 2004

From Thich Nhat Hanh's book *The World We Have* (Parallax Press, 2004).

The bells of mindfulness are sounding. All over the Earth, we are experiencing floods, drought, and massive wildfires. Sea ice is melting in the Arctic, and hurricanes and heat waves are killing thousands. The forests are fast disappearing, the deserts are growing, species are becoming extinct every day, and yet we continue to consume, ignoring the ringing bells.

All of us know that our beautiful green planet is in danger. Our way of walking on the Earth has a great influence on animals and plants. Yet we act as if our daily lives have nothing to do with the condition of the world. We are like sleepwalkers, not knowing what we are doing or where we are heading. Whether we can wake up or not depends on whether we can walk mindfully on our Mother Earth. The future of all life, including our own, depends on our mindful steps. We have to hear the bells of mindfulness that are sounding all across our planet. We have to start learning how to live in such a way that a future will be possible for our children and our grandchildren.

I have sat with the Buddha for a long time and consulted him about the issue of global warming, and the teaching of the Buddha is very clear. If we continue to live as we have been living, consuming without a thought of the future, destroying our forests and emitting dangerous amounts of carbon dioxide, then devastating climate change is inevitable. Much of our ecosystem will be destroyed. Sea levels will rise and coastal cities will be inundated, forcing hundreds of millions of refugees from their homes, creating wars and outbreaks of infectious disease.

We need a kind of collective awakening. There are among us men and women who are awakened, but it's not enough; most people are still sleeping. In my mind I see a group of chickens in a cage disputing over a few seeds of grain, unaware that in a few hours they will all be killed.

People in China, India, Vietnam, and other developing countries are still dreaming the "American dream," as if that dream were humankind's ultimate goal—having one's own car, bank account, cell phone, and television set. In twenty-five years the population of China will be 1.5 billion people, and if each of them wants to drive their own private car, China will need 99 million barrels of oil every day. But world production today is only 84 million barrels per day. So the American dream is not possible for the people of China, India, or Vietnam. The American dream is no longer possible even for the Americans. We can't continue to live like this. It's not a sustainable economy.

We have to have another dream: the dream of brotherhood and sisterhood, of loving kindness and compassion. That dream is possible right here and now. We have the Dharma, we have the means, and we have enough wisdom to be able to live this dream. Mindfulness is at the heart of awakening, of enlightenment. We practice breathing to be able to be here in the present moment so that we can recognize what is happening in and around us. If what's happening inside us is despair, we have to recognize that and act right away. We may not want to confront that mental formation, but it's a reality, and we have to recognize it in order to transform it.

We don't have to sink into despair about global warming; we can act. If we just sign a petition and forget about it, it won't help much. Urgent action must be taken at the individual and collective levels. We all have a great desire to be able to live in peace and to have environmental sustainability. What most of us don't yet have are concrete ways of making our commitment to sustainable living a reality in our daily lives. We haven't organized ourselves. We can't simply blame our governments and corporations for the chemicals that pollute our drinking water, for the violence in our neighborhoods, for the wars that destroy so many lives. It's time for each of us to wake up and take action in our own lives.

We witness violence, corruption, and destruction all around us. We all know that the laws we have in place aren't strong enough to control the cruelty and abuses of power that we see daily. Only faith and determination can keep us from falling into deep despair.

Buddhism is the strongest form of humanism we have. It can help us learn to live with responsibility, compassion, and loving kindness. Every Buddhist practitioner should be a protector of the environment. We have the power to decide the destiny of our planet. If we awaken to our true situation, there will be a change in our collective consciousness. We have to do something to wake people up. We have to help the Buddha to wake up the people who are living in a dream.

EIGHTEEN

A Letter to George W. Bush, 2006

In September 2001, Thich Nhat Hanh was in the United States leading retreats and giving public talks and interviews on his book *Anger* when the World Trade Center in New York was attacked. He led hundreds of people on walking meditation around Ground Zero and addressed the issues of nonviolence and forgiveness in a speech to more than two thousand people at New York's Riverside Church—where Dr. King had spoken nearly thirty-five years earlier about the Vietnam War. In 2003, six months after the United States invaded Iraq, Thich Nhat Hanh addressed audiences of Americans while on a teaching tour, including at the US Library of Congress, and led a two-day mindfulness retreat for US congressmen and congresswomen, where he spoke boldly for peace. He reaffirmed the importance of not demonizing the enemy and described compassion as a sign of great courage and strength—not of weakness—and the best way to guarantee true security and peace. Three years later, in 2006, with the war in Iraq now mirroring the US invasion of Vietnam, he was moved to write the following letter.

Honorable George W. Bush
The White House
Washington DC, USA

Plum Village
Le Pey 24240
Thenac, France
August 8, 2006

Dear Mr. President

Last night, I saw my brother (who died two weeks ago in the USA) coming back to me in a dream. He was with all his children. He told me, "Let's go home together." After a millisecond of hesitation, I told him joyfully, "OK, let's go."

Waking up from that dream at 5:00 AM this morning, I thought of the situation in the Middle East; and for the first time, I was able to cry. I cried for a long time, and I felt much better after about one hour. Then I went to the kitchen and made some tea. While making tea, I realized that what my brother had said is true: our home is large enough for all of us. Let us go home as brothers and sisters.

Mr. President, I think that if you could allow yourself to cry like I did this morning, you will also feel much better. It is our brothers that we kill over there. They are our brothers, God tells us so, and we also know it. They may not see us as brothers because of their anger, their misunderstanding, and their discrimination. But with some awakening, we can see things in a different way, and this will allow us to respond differently to the situation. I trust God in you; I trust Buddha nature in you.

Thank you for reading.

In gratitude and with brotherhood,

Thich Nhat Hanh
Plum Village

NINETEEN

Bat Nha: A Koan, 2010

In 2005, Vietnam's communist government granted Thich Nhat Hanh permission to return home after almost forty years of exile. The series of Thay's talks and retreats in Vietnam that followed inspired hundreds of young people to ordain as monastics, and they were welcomed at Bat Nha Monastery, a large new temple in the Central Highlands. Bat Nha Monastery grew rapidly, and because of this growth, the government reidentified Thich Nhat Hanh and his teachings as a threat to the communist regime. The Bat Nha monastics were forcibly dispersed on September 27, 2009, and in small groups sought sanctuary in the few temples willing to take the risk of sheltering them. Today, many of those same monks and nuns have become young teachers serving in the Plum Village monasteries that are thriving outside Vietnam, in Europe, America, and Asia.

This open letter was published on the Deer Park Monastery website in January 2010.

> Do not just look for what you want to see,
> that would be futile.
> Do not look for anything,
> but allow the insight to have a chance to come by itself.
> That insight will help liberate you

Bat Nha is a monastery in the central highlands of Vietnam, it is a community of monks and nuns being persecuted by the Vietnamese government, and it is the great crisis of Vietnamese Buddhism at the dawn of the twenty-first century.

A *koan* (known in Chinese as a *gong an* [公案], and in Vietnamese as a *cong an* [*công án*]) is a meditation device, a special kind of Zen riddle. Koans are solved not with the intellect but with the practice of mindfulness, concentration, and insight. A koan can be contemplated and practiced individually or collectively, but so long as it remains unsolved, a koan is unsettling. It is like an arrow piercing our body which we cannot take out; so long as it is lodged there, we can neither be happy nor at peace. Yet the koan's arrow has not really come from outside, nor is it a misfortune. A koan is an opportunity to look deeply and transcend our worries and confusion. A koan forces us to address the great questions of life, questions about our future, about the future of our country and about our own true happiness.

Some of the best known Zen koans include "The cypress in the courtyard", "If everything returns to the one, where does the one return to?", "Does a dog have Buddha nature?", and "Who is invoking the Buddha's name?" Vietnam's great leaders and statesmen have long practiced the art of contemplating koans, and contributed many famous ones of their own. Zen Master Tue Trung, whose brother General Tran Hung Dao repelled Genghis Khan's invasion, offered the powerful koan "All phenomena are impermanent. Everything that is born must finally die. What is born, and what dies?"

A koan cannot be solved by intellectual arguments, logic, or reason, nor by debates such as whether there is only mind or matter. A koan can only be solved through the power of right mindfulness and right concentration. Once we have penetrated a koan, we feel a sense of relief, and have no more fears or questioning. We see our path and realize great peace.

"Does a dog have Buddha nature?" If you think that it's the dog's problem whether or not he has Buddha nature, or if you think that it's merely a philosophical conundrum, then it's not a koan. "Where does the one return to?" If you think this is a question about the movement of an external objective reality, then that is not a koan either. If you think Bat Nha is only a problem for four hundred monks and nuns in Vietnam, a problem that simply needs a "reasonable and appropriate" solution, then that too is not a koan. Bat Nha truly becomes a koan only when you understand it as your own problem, one that deeply concerns your own happiness, your own suffering, your own future, and the future of your country and your people. If you cannot solve the koan, if you cannot sleep, eat, or work at peace, then Bat Nha has become your koan.

"Mindfulness" means to recollect something, to hold it in our heart day and night. The koan must remain in our consciousness every second, every minute of the day, never leaving us even for a moment. Mindfulness must be continuous and uninterrupted; and continuous mindfulness brings concentration. While eating, getting dressed, urinating and defecating, the practitioner needs to bring the koan to mind and look deeply into it. The koan is always at the forefront of your mind. Who is the Buddha whose name we should invoke? Who is doing the invoking? Who am I? You must find out. So long as you haven't found out you haven't made the breakthrough, you are not yet fully awake, you have not understood.

I AM A MONASTIC FROM THE BAT NHA COMMUNITY. *Bat Nha is my koan and I have the opportunity to look deeply into it in every moment of my daily life. Every day I contemplate the koan of Bat Nha—I sit with it in meditation, I walk with it in mindfulness, I am with it when I cook, when I wash my clothes, peel vegetables or sweep the floor; in every moment Bat Nha is my koan. I must produce mindfulness and concentration, because for me it is a matter of life and death, of my ideals and my future.*

We know we've been successful in our practice because despite all the oppression and harassment, many of us in our community can still laugh and be fresh as flowers. We are still able to generate peace and love, and not be dragged down by worries, fears, or hatred. Yet there are those of us who are still suffering, weighed down by the trauma of the days when Bat Nha and Phuoc Hue Temple were attacked. One of the nuns offered an insight poem to our teacher. She wrote, "The Bat Nha of yesterday has become rain, falling to the earth, sprouting the seed of awakening." This nun is barely eighteen years old, not even two years ordained, but she has successfully penetrated the koan of Bat Nha.

All we want is to practice—why can't we? The senior monks of Vietnam want to protect and sponsor us—so why does the government stop them? We don't know anything about politics, it doesn't interest us at all—so why do they keep accusing us of meddling in politics and saying Bat Nha is a threat to national security? Why was dispersing Bat Nha so important that they had to resort to using hired mobs, slander, deceit, beatings, and threats? The attackers were the age of our fathers and uncles; how could they have done that to us? If the government forbids us from living together and forces us, down to the last person, to scatter in all directions, how will our community ever be reunited? Why is it that in other countries people can practice this tradition freely, and we can't? These questions come up relentlessly and will not go away. They yearn to be answered.

During the time of sitting meditation, walking meditation, or listening to a Dharma talk; while cooking, gardening, or doing other work in mindfulness, we generate the energy of mindfulness and concentration. This energy is like fire that burns away all the haunting thoughts and questions.

The Bat Nha of yesterday was happiness. We could be true to ourselves and live the way we wanted to live. For the first time in our lives we were in an environment where we could speak openly and share our deepest thoughts and feelings with our brothers and sisters—without suspicion, without fear of betrayal. We had the opportunity as young people to serve the world, in the spirit of true brotherhood and sisterhood. This was the greatest happiness. Then Bat Nha became a nightmare, but no one will ever take from us the inner freedom we discovered there. I have found my path. Whether or not Bat Nha exists, I am no longer afraid. I can see that Bat Nha has become rain, helping the indestructible diamond seed of awakening to sprout within us. Even though we were forced from Phuoc Hue, and Bat Nha is no more, the seeds of awakening that have been planted in our hearts can never be taken away. Each one of us has to become a Bat Nha, a Phuong Boi. We know that we will make many more Bat Nha's and Phuong Boi's in the future.

We already have the seed and we already have our path, so we are no longer afraid for the future—our own, or that of our country. Tomorrow we will have the chance to help those who persecute us today. They may not see that now, but later they will understand. We know that many of those who attacked us and made us suffer have already begun to see the truth. Prejudices and wrong perceptions like those that built the Berlin Wall eventually collapse and disintegrate. There is no need to worry or despair. We can laugh as brightly as the morning sun.

I AM A CHIEF OF POLICE IN VIETNAM. *At first, I believed that the order from my superiors to wipe out Bat Nha must have been justified, that it must have been in the interests of national security. I trusted my superiors. However, as I carried out the order, I saw things that broke my heart. Bat Nha has become a koan for my life. I can't eat, I can't sleep. I toss and turn throughout the night. I ask myself, What have these people done, that I should treat them as reactionaries and threats to public safety? They seem so peaceful—but I have no peace at all. If I don't have peace in my heart, how can I keep the peace in my society?*

The young monks and nuns have not broken any laws. In fact, we were the ones who collaborated with those who seized their property. We forced them to leave the place they helped to build, where they had been living peacefully for years. We tried everything to force them out, yet they held their ground. They seemed to have so much love for each other—there seemed to be something that bound them together. They lived with such integrity. Even though they were young, none of them was pulled into smoking, drug abuse, or empty sex. They lived simply, ate vegan food, sat in meditation, listened to sutras, shared with each other, and did no harm to anyone. How can we say they are dangerous? They have never said or done anything against the government. We cannot truthfully say they are reactionaries or involved in politics. And yet we have accused them of that and driven them out by every possible means: we threatened them, we cut off their electricity and water, we went every night for many months to harass them, demanding to see their identification papers, over and over again; we did every-thing we could to break their spirit. But they never said a reproach-ful word, they offered us tea, they sang for us, and they asked to take souvenir photos with us.

In the end we hired mobs to destroy their community, to assault them and expel them. We had to be there wearing plainclothes to identify and single out the leaders so the thugs could neutralize and abduct them. Not once did they fight back. Their only weapons were chanting the Buddha's name, sitting in meditation, and locking arms to stop us from separating them as we forced them into the waiting cars. Central government even sent a Major General to coordinate the attack. Why did we need to mobilize such a massive force, from the central to the local government, to break up a group of young people with empty hands and innocent hearts?

And why did it take us more than a year to kick them out? What was there in the temple that made them so determined to stay? Every day they had just two vegan meals, three sessions of sitting meditation, one Dharma talk, and one session of walking medita-tion. Why were there so many of them, so young and yet living so harmoniously with each other? Some of them had university diplo-mas, some were sons and daughters of high-ranking officials, some had had careers and high-paying jobs; but they left it all behind for a humble life. What was so good there that it attracted so many young people? How can we just say that they were tricked by the honeyed words of a person living in the West into opposing the government?

My orders came from above and I had to obey; but I feel deeply ashamed. At first I thought they were just temporary measures, for the greater good of the country, for the sake of preserving national unity. Now I know that the whole operation was deceitful, cruel, and offensive to human conscience. I am forced to keep these thoughts to myself. I don't dare to share them with the officers in my unit, let alone my superiors. I can't go forward and I can't go back; I am a cog in a machine and I can't get out. What must I do to be true to myself?

I AM A VENERABLE OF THE BUDDHIST CHURCH OF VIETNAM. *Bat Nha haunts me night and day. I know those young monastics are practicing the true Dharma. Everyone who has come into contact with them confirms this. So why are we powerless to protect them? Why do we have to live and behave like government employees? When will I realize my dream of practicing religion without political interference? During the periods of foreign colonization, or the Diem and Thieu regimes, Buddhists faced hardships; but monastics were never as tightly controlled as they are now. What the officials want today is a Buddhism based on blind faith and rituals, not a Buddhism that offers true spiritual guidance and has the capacity to promote an ethical way of living. They are afraid of a Buddhism that offers powerful spiritual leadership and only accept religious organizations that can be controlled and manipulated. But when the Buddha was alive, he refused to submit to domination, even that of King Ajatasattu. During the French colonization and the Diem, Ky, and Thieu regimes, our ancestors fought for liberty. Why are we not continuing that work? Why have we allowed ourselves to become the instruments of a policy that is trampling our ideal of service, our noble aspiration of awakening?*

At first, I thought that if I went along with the government, I would at least have a chance to continue the "Buddha's work," whereas if I opposed the government totally, then I wouldn't be able to do anything. And so I had to silently suffer the criticism and scorn of my colleagues for being in the system. After a while, however, I saw that it was thanks to the ability and courage of those outside the Buddhist Church to voice their protests that I was permitted to do Buddhist work, albeit in a limited way. When the history of Vietnamese Buddhism is written, how will I answer for this? My aim was to revive Buddhism in order to serve the people and the nation, not to become part of a system that exists to monitor and control Buddhists.

That venerable was pressured into withdrawing his sponsorship for the monks and nuns to stay and practice at his temple. He did not have the strength to resist. He was compelled to betray his teacher and his friends and break the deep vow he made just a few years ago. It is a tragedy for him. But who is that monk? Is he someone else, or is he none other than myself? He is in me. I am also being pressured, and don't dare to do or say what I really believe in order to protect my spiritual children and young brothers and sisters. Isn't it my deepest desire to "guide the future generations and repay my debt of gratitude to the Buddha"? If so, then how can I justify the fact that I stood by helplessly and watched as the young monks and nuns, my spiritual descendents, were oppressed, humiliated, and trampled upon? How can I dare to look my spiritual children, my continuation, in the eyes? What is my true face? Who am I?

We are brothers and sisters, children of the Buddha. Is it because our practice of brotherhood is not solid enough that they have been able to divide us, that we have fallen into blaming and hating each other? According to the Buddha's teaching of non-dualism, whether we follow the Unified Buddhist Church or the Vietnam Buddhist Sangha, we are still brothers and sisters in the same family. We can do what we have to do without fighting or opposing each other, without having to consider each other as enemies. Has this enmity arisen because our practice is still weak? Has this happened because our spiritual power is not great enough? But surely we have learned a lesson: if we can accept each other and reconcile with one another, we can still resurrect our brotherhood and sisterhood, inspire the confidence of our fellow citizens, and be role models for everyone. Even though we've left it until it's too late, the situation can still be saved. Just one moment of awakening is enough to change the situation.

It seems the monks and nuns of Bat Nha have learned this lesson. Even after they were attacked and expelled they never showed any resentment toward the venerable abbot who had taken them in during these years. They knew that he was under intense pressure to force them out and that eventually he crumbled. If we in the Buddhist Church have been cornered into betraying our own brothers and sisters, it is because our spiritual integrity is not yet strong enough. How can we be wholehearted and determined enough in our daily practice to attain the spiritual strength we need? Only when we understand can we love. When we love each other we cannot see each other as enemies. As long as we see each other as enemies, we will fall prey to schemes of division and separation.

Bat Nha isn't just an issue for the Central Buddhist Church of Vietnam to resolve. Bat Nha is a koan, the challenge of our lives. How can we solve it in such a way that we are not ashamed before our ancestors? Why can't I share my thoughts and feelings with my friends in the Central Buddhist Church of Vietnam? Why aren't we allowed to harmonize our views? Why do we have to hide our thoughts and feelings?

Vietnamese Buddhists have respected and followed the Buddha, the Dharma, and the Sangha for the last two thousand years. But now groups of people were hired who wore shoes into the Buddha Hall, who put up offensive banners on the altar, who yelled and cursed and threw human excrement at venerable monks, who destroyed sacred objects, and who violently attacked, beat, and expelled monks and nuns from their temple. It was government officers who hired them, claiming they were Buddhists. This is an ugly stain on the history of Buddhism in Vietnam. It disgusts us and sickens us, yet why don't we dare to speak out? Can the Buddhist Church of Vietnam, whose members were slandered, falsely accused, and framed by the government, shake off this insult and prove the innocence of Vietnamese Buddhists?

I AM A HIGH RANKING MEMBER OF THE COMMUNIST GOVERN-MENT OF VIETNAM. *Bat Nha is an opportunity for me to look deeply at the truth and find peace in my own heart and mind. If I don't have peace, how can I have happiness? But how can I have peace, when I don't really believe in the path I walk on, and especially when I don't have faith or trust in those I call my comrades? We may be bedfellows, but are we dreaming different dreams? Why can't I share my real thoughts and feelings with those I call my comrades? Am I afraid of being denounced? Of losing my position? Why do we all have to say exactly the same things when none of us believe it? Isn't this a case of The Emperor's New Clothes, where all the members of the Emperor's court swear the Emperor is wearing a beautiful robe, when in fact he is completely naked?*

My greatest dream is for my own happiness to be in harmony with my country's. Just as trees have their roots and water has its source, our homeland has its heritage of spiritual insight. The Ly dynasty (1009–1225) was the most peaceful and compassionate dynasty in our country's history. Under the Tran dynasty (1225–1400), the People's unity was strong enough to enable them to push back attacks from the North. This unity was possible thanks to Buddhism's contribution as an inclusive and accepting spiritual path that could coexist with other spiritual and ethical traditions, such as Taoism and Confucianism, and so build a country that never needed to expel or eliminate anyone.

I've had the opportunity to study. I know Buddhism is not a theistic religion but is solidly humanist. Buddhism is open-minded and undogmatic; it has the spirit of rational inquiry. In the new century, Buddhism can go hand in hand with science. "Science" here means the spirit of scientific inquiry, the willingness to let go of old views in order to embrace new ones that are closer to reality. Modern science has gone far beyond traditional science, especially in the area of quantum physics. Is what I took for science in the past still science today? Mind and matter are just two manifestations of one reality. They contain one another and depend on one another to manifest. Modern science is putting all its energy into overcoming dualistic ways of thinking—about mind and matter, inside and outside, subject and object, space and time, mass and speed, and so on. If I am still caught in my anger, anxiety, craving, and discrimination, then my mind cannot be collected and concentrated enough to see the truth. No matter how sophisticated the instruments are that I use, behind all that technology there is still the mind that observes.

In my heart I know that the people supported the revolution so strongly because they loved their country, not an ideology. If the people's support had been based only on an ideology, and not on their deep love for the country, then we would surely have failed. I know that in the 1940s some of us, out of zealous and fanatical devotion to an ideology, crushed and assassinated revolutionaries fighting alongside us against foreign aggressors. To this day, the wounds of that time have not been healed.

As for class struggle, I should ask myself: Which class is holding power now? The proletariat or the capitalists? Is there such a thing as "The People's Capitalism," or is that just a convenient fiction?

If we want to be successful, the Party's policy must reflect the People's deep wishes. The People's deep wish is for monks and nuns to have the freedom to practice and help the world according to their ideal, in line with the laws of the land. The People's deep wish is for every citizen to be able to speak his or her mind without fear of denunciation or arrest. The People's deep wish is to separate religion from political affairs, to take the politics out of religion. If the deep wishes of the People are satisfied, then there will naturally be unity, and the Party will be supported. If the Party were in harmony with the hearts of the People, the Party would no longer need to appeal for unity or support. Such is the wish of the People. What is the policy of the Party?

I know that during the Tran and Ly dynasties, Buddhism's spirit of inclusiveness united the whole nation. Thanks to that spirit, everyone who loved their country had an opportunity to contribute to the work of building and protecting the nation, and no one was excluded. This spirit of inclusiveness in Buddhism is called "equanimity" and is one of the four Buddhist virtues, alongside loving kindness, compassion, and joy. Inclusiveness is a precious spiritual heritage, a cultural treasure. I know that during the Ly and Tran dynasties, kings and politicians practiced Buddhism just as the people did. By keeping the Buddhist precepts, following a vegetarian diet, and doing good works, they were able to earn their people's trust and confidence.

How can we eradicate the hideous social evils of drug abuse, prostitution, gambling, violence, corruption, and abuse of power, when the officials responsible for abolishing them are themselves caught up in those very evils? How can the government's policy of "cultural districts" and "cultural villages" ever be successful if it is based merely on perfunctory inspections and punishment? Who is the one that needs to be inspected and who is the one that needs to be punished?*

I know that any family that adheres to the Buddhist precepts (which we can call mindfulness trainings) enjoys peace, joy, and happiness. For the last two thousand years, Buddhism has been teaching people how to live ethical lives, be vegetarian, and keep the trainings. Following a vegetarian diet is a sign of mastery over the craving mind, of not giving in to desires. When Buddhists observe a vegetarian diet, keep the trainings, and do good deeds, they do so voluntarily and not by force or fear of punishment. At this very time, the young monks and nuns of Bat Nha are going in this direction, reinvigorating this ethical way of living. They have the potential to succeed. So why do we want to repress them and wipe them out? Are we afraid that if they have mass support, it will be at our expense? Why can't I open my heart to practice like them, to be one with them and benefit from their support? Why can't we do as the kings of the Tran and Ly dynasties did? Just because we are

---

* "During my first trip back to our country in 2005, I saw banners which read 'cultural town,' 'cultural village,' 'cultural area,' etc. I was quietly happy, thinking that this was an intelligent and prompt policy of the government. Asking about it, I learned that the policy of forming those cultural towns and areas was to address the already spreading social evils such as drug addiction, prostitution, gambling, violence, etc. After being in Vietnam for a month, I was told that the government did not succeed much with those cultural towns and areas. They were only words, but not truths. The methods to control and to punish were not enough to dispel the social evils, especially when the people who carry out the control and punishment are also caught in social evils such as corruption, power abuse, and treachery."—From "Bat Nha: The Indestructible Seed of Awakening," published on the Plum Village website in late 2009.

Marxists, does that mean we don't have the right to take refuge in the Buddha, Dharma, and Sangha, to be vegetarian and practice the mindfulness trainings?

I know that in the party and in the government, many people now claim to be open minded toward religion and spirituality. In fact, all the top officials believe in things like feng shui, destiny, psychic powers, and even the idea of extending one person's lifespan by transferring life years from someone else. They have gone from one extreme to another. And yet they outwardly claim not to be superstitious.

The Ly and Tran kings truly believed in a path of virtue and spirituality. Many of them lived exemplary ethical lives, and the people had confidence in them and were inspired to do the same. One king knew how to practice the mindfulness trainings, followed a vegetarian diet, sent blankets to prisons, and went out into towns and villages to meet the people and see the truth of how they lived and what they suffered. A king who knows how to do sitting meditation, look deeply into koans, practice beginning anew six times daily,* write commentaries on sutras, take refuge in the wise counsel of a Zen master whom he respects as the national teacher, and yield the throne to his son in order to become a simple monk on Yen Tu mountain—such a king can be a great example of morality for the whole nation.

Nowadays we're always urging government officials and each other to "study and follow the virtuous example of Ho Chi Minh." But who is the one that is living a good example for their comrades? Mahayana Buddhism teaches that "You have to be that person. You

---

* In this context, to begin anew is to look deeply and honestly at ourselves, our past actions, speech, and thoughts, and to create a fresh beginning within ourselves and in our relationships.

have to be the role model. You have to live that way yourself. Only then will you give others the inspiration to do the same." I have to be that person. I know that corruption and abuse of power have become a national catastrophe. We have been lamenting this for so many years already, and yet the situation just gets worse with every passing day. Why? Is it because I'm only able to proudly boast of my ancestors' glorious past, and am not in fact able to do as they did? And today, when there are young people actually doing it, why do we block and suppress them?

The Bat Nha situation may have started with a travel agency owned by a high police officer. Soon it involved hotels, then visas, and eventually the abuse of power and the exercise of revenge. Now it has become a policy the whole country has to follow. Maybe I have not taken the time to examine this. I just go along with the false reports and casually allow the people I am supervising to use lies, deception, and oppression against these gentle people who never have caused any disturbance to society. In the end I am put in a position where I become the enemy of the very things I once cherished. Are my true enemies really outside of me? My enemies are within. Do I have enough courage and intelligence to face my own weaknesses? That is the fundamental question.

The Plum Village practices offer a rare opportunity to modernize Buddhism in Vietnam; the last four years have proved their effectiveness. Why are we allowing ourselves to be pressured by our powerful neighbor into persecuting and destroying such a precious living treasure?* What will we get that is so precious, in return for destroying this treasure we already have?

---

* During a 2008 interview on Italian television, Thich Nhat Hanh made some statements about the Dalai Lama that upset Chinese officials, who in turn put pressure on the Vietnamese government to close Bat Nha.

The best way to celebrate the thousand-year anniversary of Hanoi is to strive to practice, to live like our great ancestors Ly Cong Uan, Tran Thai Tong, Tran Thanh Tong, Truc Lam Dai Si, and Master Tue Trung. They were politicians, but at the same time lived a true spiritual life that they believed in. What have I to be proud of, other than the legends of my ancestors? I have lost my revolutionary ideal. I have snuffed out the sacred flame of my deepest aspiration. My comrades are no longer truly my comrades because their own sacred flame of revolutionary idealism has been extinguished. They are only in the Party out of self-interest, for fame and status. The Plum Village tradition is part of my country's cultural heritage and is contributing to a global cultural ethic—not just in theory but, most importantly, in practice. So many people all around the world have heard about this tradition and are benefiting from these teachings. I should be proud of this, so why did I allow the tradition to be attacked and wiped out in the very land where it was born? These are the questions that, if allowed to penetrate and act upon the depths of my consciousness, can awaken the wisdom within. This will give me the insight I need to see the path and way out I have been longing for.

I AM A HEAD OF STATE OR FOREIGN MINISTER. *My country is or is not a member of the Security Council or the UN Commission on Human Rights. I know that events like Bat Nha, Tam Toa, Tiananmen Square, and the annexation of Tibet are serious violations of Human Rights. But because of national interest, because our country wants to continue to do business with them, because we want to sell arms, airplanes, fast trains, nuclear power plants, and other technologies, because we want a market for our products, I cannot express myself frankly and make real decisions that can create pressure on that country to stop violating human rights.*

I feel ashamed. My conscience is not at peace but because I want my party and my government to succeed, I tell myself that these violations are not serious enough for my country to take a stance. It seems that I too am caught in a system, a kind of machinery, and I cannot really be myself. I'm not able to give voice to my real feelings or to speak out about the situation. What do I have to do to get the peace that I so badly need? Bat Nha is of course a situation in Vietnam, but it has also become a koan for a high-ranking political leader like me. What path can I take in order to really be myself?

—

The koan "Bat Nha" is everyone's koan; it is the koan of every individual and every community. The koan can be practiced by a Bat Nha monastic, by a monk or nun studying at a Buddhist Institute in Vietnam, a Venerable in the Buddhist Church of Vietnam, a police officer, a Head of Department, a Catholic priest, a Protestant minister, a Politburo member, a Chairman of a city's People's Committee, a Provincial Party Secretary, a member of the Central Committee, a newspaper or magazine editor, an intellectual, an artist, a businessperson, a teacher, a journalist, an abbot or abbess, an international political leader or ambassador. Bat Nha is an opportunity, because Bat Nha can help you see clearly what you couldn't—or didn't want—to see before.

In the Zen tradition, there are retreats of seven, twenty-one, and forty-nine days. During these retreats, the practitioner invests their whole heart and mind into the koan. Every moment of their daily life is also a moment of looking deeply: when sitting, walking, breathing, eating, brushing their teeth, or washing their clothes. At every moment the mind is concentrated on the koan. The most popular retreat is the seven-day retreat. Every day the practitioner gets the chance to interact with the Zen master in the direct guidance session. The Zen master offers guidance to help the practitioner direct their concentration in the correct way, opening up their mind and helping them to see, showing them the situation so the truth can reveal itself clearly.*

In the direct guidance sessions the truth is not transmitted from master to practitioner. Practitioners must realize the truth for themselves. The Zen master may give about ten minutes of guidance, to open your mind and point things out, and then everyone returns to their own sitting place to continue to look deeply. Sometimes there are hundreds of practitioners, all sitting together in the meditation hall, facing the wall. After a period of sitting meditation, there is a period of walking meditation. Practitioners walk slowly, each and every step bringing them back to the koan. At meal times, practitioners may eat at their meditation cushion. While eating they contemplate the koan. Urinating and defecating are also opportunities to look deeply. Noble silence is essential for meditative enquiry, and that is why outside the meditation hall there is always a sign that reads "Noble Silence."

In the past, King Tran Thai Tong (1218–1277) became enlightened by investigating the two koans "Four mountains" and "A true person has no position."† Zen master Lieu Quan (1670–1742)

---

* Practicing with a koan in this way is not a typical component of Plum Village retreats.

† Long ago, Vietnam's King Tran Thai Tong practiced Zen. He meditated on koans and contributed forty new koans, as well as various invocations, recitations, and short verses, for friends to practice with him at the palace's True Teachings Temple. These koans have been recorded in his book, *Instructions on Emptiness*. Master Tue Trung, a lay man, composed thirteen of his own koans, which are recorded in the Record of Zen Master Tue Trung. *The Blue Cliff Record*, edited by Zen master Yuan Wu in the twelfth century, has over one hundred koans complete with teachings, commentaries and guidelines. This classic has been used by Zen practitioners for centuries.

became enlightened thanks to his practice of the koan "The all proceeds to the one; where does the one go?" He presented his insight at Tu Dam Temple in the city of Hue, Vietnam.

If you want to be successful in your practice of koans, you must be able to let go of all intellectual knowledge, all notions, and all points of view you currently hold. If you are caught in a personal opinion, standpoint, or ideology, you do not have enough freedom to allow the koan's insight to break forth into your consciousness. You have to release everything you have encountered before, everything you have previously taken to be the truth. As long as you believe you already hold the truth in your hand, the door to your mind is closed. Even if the truth comes knocking, you will not be able to receive it. Present knowledge is an obstacle. Buddhism demands freedom. Freedom of thought is the basic condition for progress. It is the true spirit of science. It is precisely in that space of freedom that the flower of wisdom can bloom.

In the Zen tradition, community is a very positive element. When hundreds of practitioners silently look deeply together, the collective energy of mindfulness and concentration is very powerful. This collective energy nourishes your concentration in every minute and every second, giving you the opportunity to have a breakthrough in your practice of the koan. This kind of environment is very different from that of a conference, discussion, or meeting. The firm discipline of your meditation practice, the favorable environment for concentration, as well as the guidance of the Zen master and silent support of fellow practitioners, all provide you with many opportunities to succeed.

The suggestions given above can be seen as direct guidance to help you in your practice of looking deeply. You have to see these words as an instrument, not as the truth. They are the raft that can bring you to the other shore; they are not the shore itself. Once you reach the other shore, you have to abandon the raft. If you are successful in looking deeply, you will have freedom, you will be able to see your path. Then you can just burn these words, or throw them away.

I wish you all success in the work of looking deeply into the Bat Nha koan.

TWENTY

Twelve Proposals to Celebrate Hanoi's 1,000 Years

On October 10, 2010 (10/10/10), the city of Hanoi marked its thousand-year anniversary. In June of that year, Thich Nhat Hanh published the following twelve progressive proposals for the city, which would support the continuation of Vietnamese Buddhist culture.

In the year 1010, one thousand years ago, the first king of the Ly dynasty founded Thang Long, the city now known as Hanoi. The Ly dynasty has been described as "the most compassionate, peaceful and harmonious in the history of Vietnam" by the eminent twentieth century Vietnamese historian Hoang Xuan Han. This, he wrote, was "thanks to the influence of Buddhism."

The first king of the Ly dynasty was Ly Thai To. From a very young age he had been trained as a Buddhist monastic aspirant at Luc To temple by Zen Master Van Hanh. When he ascended to the throne, he organized political and cultural life in the spirit of openness, fearlessness, and nondualism as taught by Zen Master Van Hanh. The practice of Buddhism gave the nation a solid foundation of peace and happiness which lasted for centuries. Ly Nhah Tong, the fourth king in the Ly Dynasty, spoke of Master Van Hanh with great respect. "Master Van Hanh's actions embraced the whole of the past, present and future," he said. "His words presaged events with extraordinary accuracy. In his hometown, the northern village of Co Phap, he needed only to plant his staff in the ground and sit in stillness, and the city of Thang Long could enjoy stability and peace forever."

> Ten thousand actions embrace past, present and future
> Words of foretelling are effective
> With a monk's staff firmly planted in Co Phap
> Stability reigns in the kingdom

Twelve Proposals

The best way to celebrate one thousand years of Hanoi is for the government and the whole nation to endeavor to take up and continue the work our forefathers began in founding the capital, namely:

1. *Establish a university with the name Van Hanh**

> Offering courses that have the capacity to transmit the spirit of openness, fearlessness, and non-dualism, as taught by Master Van Hanh (937–1018). Similar universities can be established simultaneously in other major cities of the country.

---

* The Zen Master's name "Van Hanh" means "Ten Thousand Actions;" The Zen Master's name "Nhat Hanh" means "One Action." Thich Nhat Hanh founded a "Van Hanh Buddhist University" in Saigon in the early 1960s.

2. *Allocate time for the daily study of global ethics at all levels of education*

Investing money in training teachers to teach applied ethics, in the light of both traditional Vietnamese cultural values and global ethics. The classes should offer concrete practices that can be applied to address contemporary social issues such as domestic violence, divorce, suicide, drug abuse, prostitution, abuse of power, and corruption. In this way, the policy of model ethical towns and villages can be realized.

3. *Call for a summit of all religious traditions and charitable organizations in Vietnam to draft a non-sectarian Charter of Ethics*

This can serve as a basis for the practice of ethics throughout the country. This text should have the capacity to bring about a healthy and compassionate society and save the planet. Each tradition should present and contribute their own ethical code (for example, Buddhism would present the Revised Five Mindfulness Trainings) and together discuss, exchange, and learn from one another how these principles can be applied in family life, schools, and workplaces.* Recitations of the resulting non-sectarian text can be organized once a month in every temple, church, town hall, or library. Government officials should also attend recitations alongside ordinary citizens.

---

* The Five Mindfulness Trainings are Thich Nhat Hanh's modernization of the Five Precepts offered by the Buddha. They represent a nonsectarian way to bring mindfulness into every area of daily life.

4. *Establish councils of wise and ethical people in villages, towns, and cities*

These councils should be composed of people renowned for their kindness and virtue, who can be ethical role models for the community. The councils could include Catholic priests, Protestant Ministers, and Buddhist Abbots and Abbesses, who would care for the ethical wellbeing of the community with their wisdom, loving kindness, encouragement, and firmness.

5. *Offer an amnesty for all those in exile abroad, banished from their hometown within Vietnam or imprisoned*

... whether for being members of unauthorized organizations or churches or because they have called for pluralism, multipartyism, freedom of religion, or freedom of speech. A number of prisoners should be given early release on social work under the guidance and sponsorship of ordained members of all religions.

6. *Repeal taxes for anyone without a home, without a job, or source of income.*

7. *Establish Sundays as a "No Car Day" in Hanoi and other big cities and towns*

Citizens should only use bicycles, rickshaws, horse carriages, or walk, except in emergencies. Sundays should also be a "No Smoking Day" and "No Alcohol Day"—a day on which no cigarettes, wine, or beer are sold.

8. *Support the establishment of vegetarian restaurants*

In the capital and other major cities, every restaurant must offer at least a few vegetarian dishes on the menu, and everyone should be encouraged to be vegetarian for at least fifteen days a month (according to the UN's recommendations to cut back meat consumption by 50 percent to save the planet). Those who fully embrace a vegetarian diet can benefit from a 50 percent discount on their health insurance contributions.

9. *Subsidize solar energy*

. . . for cooking rice, boiling water, lighting, preparing tea, washing clothes, and so on.

10. *End the production and use of plastic bags and packaging*

11. *Call for a Great Buddhist Summit*

Invite Venerable monks and nuns from inside and outside the country to re-establish a People's Buddhist Church, totally free from political interference.

12. *Organize retreats in Vietnam*

For Vietnamese people and foreigners to learn and practice ways to transform violence and build brotherhood and sisterhood in the spirit of openness and non-dualism as taught by Zen Master Van Hanh.

If the government, lawmakers, and law-enforcers of the country do not want to, or cannot, realize these proposals, then we, the People, will do it by ourselves, beginning with the Buddhists and with the support of other religions and charitable associations.

TWENTY-ONE

The Ancient Tree, 1988

Thich Nhat Hanh says "The Ancient Tree" was written as "a memorial to Nhat Chi Mai, my student who immolated herself for peace on May 16, 1967."*

In a deep forest in the highlands stood an ancient tree. No one knew how many thousands of years it had lived. Its trunk was so large that the arm spans of eighteen people could not embrace it; great roots pushed up through the ground and spread to a radius of fifty meters. The earth beneath the tree's shadow was unusually cool. Its bark was as hard as rock; if you pressed a fingernail against it, pain ran through your finger. Its branches held tens of thousands of nests, sheltering hundreds of thousands of birds, both large and small.

In the morning, when the sun rose, the first rays of light were like a conductor's baton, initiating a mighty symphony: the voices

---

* Nhat Chi Mai (1934–1967) was active in the School of Youth for Social Service and was one of the six original Order of Interbeing members, ordained in 1966. In a letter to Thich Nhat Hanh written just before she died, Nhat Chi Mai reassured him: "Teacher, Don't you worry too much. Peace will come soon."

of thousands of birds, a symphony as majestic as the sun dawning behind the summit of the mountain. All the creatures of the mountain and forest arose, either on two feet or four, slowly, in wonder.

In the great tree there was a hole as large as a grapefruit from Bien Hoa (a region of Vietnam gamed for its large grapefruits) twelve meters from the ground. In the hole lay a small brown egg. No one could say if a bird had brought the beautiful egg to the hole. Some thought the egg had not come from a living bird but had been forged by the sacred air of the forest and the life energy of the great tree.

Thirty years passed; the egg remained intact. Some nights, birds would be startled from their sleep by a cloud hovering over the hole and a brilliant light shining there, illuminating an entire corner of the forest. Finally, one night, under a full moon, the egg opened, and a strange bird was born. The bird was very little; it gave a small chirp in the cold night. The moon was very bright; the stars were very bright. The tiny bird cried throughout the night. Its cry was neither tragic nor bold; it was a cry of surprise and strangeness. It cried until the sun appeared. The first rays of light opened the symphony; thousands of birds' voices broke forth. From that moment, the little bird cried no more.

It grew quickly. The nuts and grains mother birds brought to the hole were always plenty. Soon the hole in the tree became too small, and the bird had to find another place, much larger, in which to live. It now knew how to fly; it looked for its own food and gathered sticks of straw to cover the floor of its new nest. Strangely, although the egg had been brown, the bird was as white as snow. When it flew, its wingspan was vast, and it moved slowly and very quietly. Often it flew to faraway places where white waterfalls tumbled day and night like the majestic breath of the earth and sky.

Sometimes the bird did not return for several days. When it returned, it lay in its nest all day and night, thoughtfully and quietly. Its two eyes were very bright; they never lost the look of surprise they had from the beginning.

Now, in the ancient forest of Dai Lao, a hermit's small hut stood on the slope of a hill.* There a monk had lived for almost fifty years. The bird often flew across Dai Lao forest; from time to time it saw the monk slowly walking down the path to the spring, holding a water jug in his hand. One day, smoke gently lingered over the roof of the humble hut, and an atmosphere of warmth surrounded the hill. The bird saw two monks together on the path leading from the spring to the hut, speaking as they walked. That night the bird remained in Dai Lao forest. Concealed in the branches of a tree, the bird watched the light of the fire flickering inside the hut, where the two monks conversed through the night.

The bird flew high, high over the ancient forest. For several days it flew back and forth in the sky without landing. Below stood the great tree in the ancient forest; below, the creatures of the mountain and forest were concealed by grass, bushes, and trees. Since the day the bird listened to the exchange between the two monks, its bewilderment grew. Where have I come from and where will I go? How many thousands of years will the great tree stand?

The bird had heard the two monks speak about Time. What is Time? Why has Time brought us here, and why will it take us away? The nut which a bird eats has its own delicious nature. How can I find out the nature of Time? The bird wanted to pick up a small

---

* Dai Lao, also known as B'Lao, is located in Vietnam's central highlands. It is where Thich Nhat Hanh and friends built the forest hermitage Phuong Boi in the late 1950s.

piece of Time and lie quietly with it in its nest for several days to examine its nature. Even if it took months or years to examine, the bird was willing.

The bird flew high, high over the ancient forest. It was like a round balloon drifting in nothingness. The bird felt its nature was as empty as a balloon's. The emptiness of its nature was the ground of its existence, but it was also the cause of the bird's suffering. "Time, if I could find you, certainly I could find myself," thought the bird.

After several days and nights, the bird came to rest quietly in its nest. It had brought back a tiny piece of earth from the Dai Lao forest. Deep in thought, it picked up the piece of earth to examine it. The monk from the Dai Lao forest had said to his friend, "Time is stilled in Eternity. There Love and beloved are One. Each blade of grass, each piece of earth, each leaf, is one with that love."

The bird was still unable to find Time. The small token of earth from the Dai Lao forest revealed nothing. Perhaps the monk had lied to his friend. Time lies in Love, but where is Love? The bird remembered the splashing waterfalls endlessly tumbling in the Northwest Forest. It remembered the days it listened to the sound of the waterfalls from morning to evening. The bird had imagined itself tumbling like a waterfall. It played with the light shining on the water; it caressed the pebbles and rocks in the streams. In those moments, the bird felt that it was the waterfall itself, that the sound of endless falling water came from it.

One noon, flying across the Dai Lao Forest, the bird did not see the hut. The whole forest had burned; only a pile of ashes remained where the monk's hut had been. In a panic, the bird flew around searching. The monk was no longer in the forest. Where had he gone? Corpses of animals. Corpses of birds. Had the fire consumed the monk? The bird was bewildered. Time, what are you? Why do you bring us here, and why will you take us away? The monk said, "Time is stilled in Eternity." If that is so, perhaps Love has returned the monk to Itself.

Suddenly the bird felt anxious. It flew swiftly back to the ancient forest. Anguished cries of many birds. Explosions. The ancient forest, far away, was burning. Faster, faster still, the bird flew. The fire licked the sky. The fire spread near the great tree. Hundreds of thousands of birds shrieked in fright.

The fire approached the great tree. The bird fanned the fire with its wings, hoping to put it out, but the fire burned more fiercely. The bird sped to the spring, dipped its wings in the water, and rushed back to shake the water over the forest. The drops sizzled. It was not enough, not enough. The bird's entire body soaked in water was not enough to extinguish the fire.

Cries of hundreds of thousands of birds. Screams of young birds without feathers to fly. The fire began to burn the great tree. Why was there no rain? Why didn't the downpour that fell endlessly in the Northwest Forest flow like a waterfall? The bird let forth a piercing cry. The cry was tragic and passionate and was suddenly transformed into the rushing sound of a waterfall. All at once, the bird felt the fullness of its existence. Loneliness and emptiness vanished like an illusion. The image of the monk. The image of the sun behind the mountain peak. The image of rushing water falling endlessly through a thousand lifetimes. The cry of the bird was now the full sound of the waterfall. Without anxiety, the bird plunged into the forest fire like a majestic waterfall.

The next morning was calm. The marvelous rays of the sun shone, but there was no symphony, no voices of tens of thousands of birds. Portions of the forest were completely burned. The great tree still stood, but more than half of its branches and leaves were charred. Corpses of large birds, corpses of small birds. The morning forest was silent.

The birds still alive called one another, their voices bewildered. They did not know by what grace the clear sky had suddenly poured forth rain, extinguishing the forest fire the afternoon before. They remembered seeing the bird shaking water from its two wings. They knew it was the white bird from the great tree. They flew everywhere throughout the forest seeking the corpse of the white bird, but they did not find it.

Perhaps the bird had flown away to live in a different forest. Perhaps the bird had been killed by the fire. The great tree, its body covered with wounds, did not say a word. The birds cocked their heads to the sky and began to build new nests in the wounded body of the great tree. Does the great tree miss the child which sacred mountain air and the life energy of four thousand years had given birth to? Bird, where have you gone? Listen to the monk: I believe Time has returned the bird to the Love which is the source of all things.

Part I

"The Path of Return Continues the Journey" was first published in 1972
by Hoa Binh Press, New York, as a booklet. It was translated
from the Vietnamese by Vo-Dinh Mai and Jim Forest.

Part II

1. "Love in Action" is adapted from the booklet *Love in Action: The Nonviolent Struggle for Peace in Vietnam* (Paris: Vietnamese Buddhist
Peace Delegation, 1969).

2. "A Proposal for Peace" was read at a press conference in Washington,
DC, on June 1, 1966, and reprinted in the Congressional Record,
June 2, 1966, pp. A3001–A3003.

3. "Our Green Garden" is from *The New York Review of Books,* June 9,
1966.

4. "The Menton Statement: A Message to Our 3.5 Billion Neighbors on
Planet Earth" was first published in the *UNESCO Courier,* July
1971.

5. "From Weapons to Human Solidarity" is adapted from a speech given
in the United States in 1971.

6. "On Simplicity" is from "The Montagnards' Way of Simplicity" printed in the Fellowship of Reconciliation's *Fellowship* magazine (Nyack, New York), March 1975, pp. 10–12.

7. "The Human Family" is adapted from a talk entitled "Man and Nature," given at the World Federation of Mental Health World Congress in Copenhagen, August 1975, and was previously printed in Fred Eppsteiner (ed.), The *Path of Compassion: Writings on Socially Engaged Buddhism* (Berkeley: Parallax Press, 1988), pp. 40–46.

8. "I Have Lost My Brother" is from a talk given at the Reverence for Life Conference, New York, June 9, 1982, and from *Le Lotus*, the newsletter of the Vietnamese Buddhist Peace Delegation, Paris, December 1, 1973.

9. "Call Me by My True Names" is from a talk given at the Rochester Zen Center, May 1983, previously published in *The Path of Compassion* (Berkeley: Parallax Press, 2008), pp. 31–39.

10. "Ahimsa: The Path of Harmlessness" is from two talks given at Plum Village, France in August 1988.

11. "If You Want Peace, Peace Is with You Immediately" is from The Sun *My Heart* (Berkeley: Parallax Press, 1988), pp. 123–125.

12. "To Veterans" is from the talks given during retreats for veterans at Casa de Maria, Santa Barbara, California in May 1989 and Omega Institute, Rhinebeck, New York in June 1991.

13. "A Peaceful Heart" is from a talk given at Plum Village in March 1991.

14. "The Roots of War" is from a series of talks given in North America, Spring 1991, and from an interview by Tami Simon in Houston, Texas, in March 1991.

15. "The Sun My Heart" is from "The Last Tree" in Allan Hunt Badiner (ed.), *Dharma Gaia* (Berkeley: Parallax Press, 1991), pp. 217–221, and from *The Mindfulness Bell*, Berkeley, California, Summer

1992, pp. 1–6. Parts of this essay are also found in *The Sun My Heart* (Berkeley: Parallax Press, 2020).

16. "The Way Ahead for Buddhism in Vietnam" was printed in *The Mindfulness Bell*, Spring 1993, pp. 2 and 31.

17. "The Bells of Mindfulness." *The World We Have* (Berkeley, CA: Parallax Press, 2004), pp. 1–5.

18. "A Letter to George W. Bush," 2006.

19. "Bat Nha: A Koan," 2010.

20. "Twelve Proposals to Celebrate Hanoi's 1,000 Years," 2010.

21. "The Ancient Tree" is from *The Pine Gate* (Buffalo, New York: White Pine Press, 1988).

ABOUT THICH NHAT HANH

Thich Nhat Hanh is one of the most revered and influential spiritual teachers in the world today. Born in Vietnam in 1926, he became a Zen Buddhist monk at the age of sixteen. Over seven decades of teaching, he has published more than one hundred books, which have sold more than four million copies in the United States alone. Exiled from Vietnam in 1966 for promoting peace, his teachings on Buddhism as a path to social and political transformation are responsible for bringing the mindfulness movement to Western culture. He established the international Plum Village Community of Engaged Buddhism in France, now the largest Buddhist monastery in Europe and the heart of a growing community of practice centers around the world. He passed away in 2022 at the age of ninety-five at his root temple, Tu Hieu, in Hue, Vietnam.

Monastics and visitors practice the art of mindful living in the tradition of Thich Nhat Hanh at our mindfulness practice centers around the world. To reach any of these communities, or for information about how individuals, couples, and families can join in a retreat, please contact:

PLUM VILLAGE
33580 Dieulivol, France
plumvillage.org

LA MAISON DE L'INSPIR
77510 Villeneuve-sur-Bellot, France
maisondelinspir.org

HEALING SPRING
MONASTERY
77510 Verdelot, France
healingspringmonastery.org

MAGNOLIA GROVE
MONASTERY
Batesville, MS 38606, USA
magnoliagrovemonastery.org

BLUE CLIFF MONASTERY
Pine Bush, NY 12566, USA
bluecliffmonastery.org

DEER PARK MONASTERY
Escondido, CA 92026, USA
deerparkmonastery.org

EUROPEAN INSTITUTE OF
APPLIED BUDDHISM
D-51545 Waldbröl, Germany
eiab.eu

THAILAND PLUM VILLAGE
Nakhon Ratchasima
30130 Thailand
thaiplumvillage.org

ASIAN INSTITUTE OF
APPLIED BUDDHISM
Lantau Island, Hong Kong
pvfhk.org

STREAM ENTERING
MONASTERY
Beaufort, Victoria 3373
Australia
nhapluu.org

MOUNTAIN SPRING
MONASTERY
Bilpin, NSW 2758, Australia
mountainspringmonastery.org

For more information visit: *plumvillage.org*
To find an online sangha visit: *plumline.org*
For more resources, try the Plum Village app: *plumvillage.app*
Social media: *@thichnhathanh @plumvillagefrance*

PARALLAX PRESS, a nonprofit publisher founded by Zen Master Thich Nhat Hanh, publishes books and media on the art of mindful living and Engaged Buddhism. We are committed to offering teachings that help transform suffering and injustice. Our aspiration is to contribute to collective insight and awakening, bringing about a more joyful, healthy, and compassionate society.

View our entire library at parallax.org.

THE MINDFULNESS BELL is a journal of the art of mindful living in the Plum Village tradition of Thich Nhat Hanh. To subscribe or to see the worldwide directory of Sanghas (local mindfulness groups), visit mindfulnessbell.org.